Presented to:

By:

Date:

Occasion:

This book in its entirety—from literary development to artwork and final design—
is a creation of Koechel Peterson & Associates. Artwork by Katia Andreeva is
reproduced under license from Koechel Peterson & Associates and may not be
reproduced without permission. For information regarding art prints featured in
this book, please contact: Koechel Peterson & Associates, 2600 East 26th Street,
Minneapolis, Minnesota, 55406, 1-612-721-5017.

Being the Person God Made You to Be, Warner Books Edition, copyright © 2001
by Joyce Meyer, Life in the Word, Inc., P.O. Box 655, Fenton, Missouri, 63026.
All rights reserved.
First Warner Faith printing: October 2002

The Power of Determination, copyright © 2003 by Joyce Meyer. All rights reserved.
First Warner Faith printing: May 2003

Compilation copyright © 2004 by Joyce Meyer. All rights reserved.
First Warner Faith printing: June 2004

Warner Faith

Time Warner Book Group
1271 Avenue of the Americas, New York, NY 10020
Visit our Web site at www.twbookmark.com

The Warner Faith name and logo are registered trademarks of Warner Books.

Printed in Singapore

ISBN: 0-446-57757-X

10 9 8 7 6 5 4 3 2 1

BEING THE PERSON GOD MADE YOU TO BE

THE POWER OF DETERMINATION

JOYCE MEYER

WARNER
Faith

New York • Boston • Nashville

CONTENTS

BEING THE PERSON
GOD MADE YOU TO BE

CONTENTS

CONTENTS

THE POWER OF DETERMINATION

CONTENTS

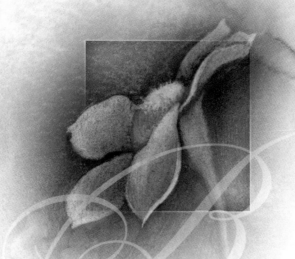

Being the
Person God
Made You to Be

SELF-ACCEPTANCE

You will never sense fulfillment in life unless you reach the goal of being yourself. Don't be in competition with others; just concentrate on fulfilling your potential.

GOD'S WORD FOR YOU

May Christ through your faith [actually] dwell (settle down, abide, make His permanent home) in your hearts! May you be rooted deep in love and founded securely on love.

EPHESIANS 3:17

one

SELF-ACCEPTANCE

During my years of ministry, I have discovered that most people really don't like themselves. This is a very big problem, much bigger than one might think initially. It is certainly not God's will for His children to feel this way. Rather, it is a part of Satan's attempt to ruin us.

If we don't get along with ourselves, we won't get along with other people. When we reject ourselves, it may seem to us that others reject us as well. Relationships are a vital part of our lives. How we feel about ourselves is a determining factor in our success in life and in relationships.

Our self-image is the inner picture we carry of ourselves. If what we see is not healthy, not true to the Scriptures, we will suffer from fear, insecurity, and various misconceptions about ourselves. For many years, it devastated my own life.

God is a God of hearts. He sees our heart, not just the exterior shell we live in (the flesh) that seems to get us into so much trouble. Our Father in heaven never intended for us to feel bad about ourselves. He wants us to know ourselves and yet accept ourselves in the same way that He does.

Jesus came to bring restoration to our lives.
One of the things He came to restore
is a healthy, balanced self-image.

GOD'S WORD FOR YOU

And God saw everything that He had made, and behold, it was very good (suitable, pleasant) and He approved it completely. And there was evening and there was morning, a sixth day.

GENESIS 1:31

THE ROOT OF REJECTION

Rejection starts as a seed that is planted in our lives through different things that happen to us. The devil does not want to plant just a seed of rejection. He wants to plant it deep so it will develop into a root that will go way down and have other little rootlets attached to it. Eventually these roots and rootlets will become a tree.

Whatever you are rooted in will determine the fruit in your life—good or bad. If you are rooted in rejection, abuse, shame, guilt, or a poor self-image —if you are rooted in thinking, *Something is wrong with me!*—your "tree" will bear depression, negativism, a lack of confidence, anger, hostility, a controlling spirit, judgmentalism, a chip on the shoulder, hatred, and self-pity. It leads you to say to yourself, "Well, the real me is not acceptable, so I need to produce a *pretend me!*"

All the areas of your life that are out of order can be reconciled through Jesus and the work that He has done on the cross. It happened to me, and God can do it for you. Begin to believe it! Don't settle for bondage, but be determined to be free!

Here is the good news—you can be delivered from the power of rejection!

GOD'S WORD FOR YOU

. . . God's love has been poured out in our hearts through the Holy Spirit Who has been given to us.

ROMANS 5:5

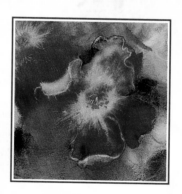

GODLY SELF-LOVE

The Bible teaches us that the love of God has been poured out in our hearts by the Holy Spirit Who has been given to us. That simply means that when the Lord, in the person of the Holy Spirit, comes to dwell in our heart because of our faith in His Son Jesus Christ, He brings love with Him, because God is love (1 John 4:8).

We all need to ask ourselves what we are doing with the love of God that has been freely given to us. Are we rejecting it because we don't think we are valuable enough to be loved? Do we believe God is like other people who have rejected and hurt us? Or are we receiving His love by faith, believing that He is greater than our failures and weaknesses?

We should love ourselves—not in a selfish, self-centered way that produces a lifestyle of self-indulgence, but in a balanced, godly way, a way that simply affirms God's creation as essentially good and right.

God's plan is this: He wants us to receive His love, love ourselves in a godly way, generously love Him in return, and finally love all the people who come into our lives.

When God reaches out to love us,
He is attempting to start a cycle that will
bless not only us but also many others.

GOD'S WORD FOR YOU

And Mephibosheth son of Jonathan, the son of Saul, came to David and fell on his face and did obeisance. David said, Mephibosheth! And he answered, Behold your servant!

David said to him, Fear not, for I will surely show you kindness for Jonathan your father's sake, and will restore to you all the land of Saul your father [grandfather], and you shall eat at my table always.

And [the cripple] bowed himself and said, What is your servant, that you should look upon such a dead dog as I am?

2 SAMUEL 9:6-8

THE DEAD-DOG IMAGE

Mephibosheth was the grandson of King Saul and the son of Jonathan, who had been a close covenant friend to David. Crippled as a youth, Mephibosheth had a poor self-image, a dead-dog image. Instead of seeing himself as the rightful heir to his father's and grandfather's legacy, he saw himself as someone who would be rejected.

When David sent for Mephibosheth, he fell down before the king and displayed fear. David told him not to fear, that he intended to show him kindness. Mephibosheth's response is an important example of the kind of poor self-image we all need to overcome.

A poor self-image causes us to operate in fear instead of faith. We look at what is wrong with us instead of what is right with Jesus. He has taken our wrongness and given us His righteousness (2 Corinthians 5:21). We need to walk in the reality of that truth.

I love the end of the story. David blessed Mephibosheth for Jonathan's sake. He gave him servants and land and provided for all of his needs.

I relate Mephibosheth's lameness to our own weaknesses. We may also fellowship and eat with our King Jesus—despite our faults and weaknesses.

We have a covenant with God, sealed and ratified in the blood of Jesus Christ.

GOD'S WORD FOR YOU

There we saw the Nephilim [or giants], the sons of Anak, who come from the giants; and we were in our own sight as grasshoppers, and so we were in their sight.

NUMBERS 13:33

Are You a Grasshopper?

We read in Numbers 13 of how Moses sent twelve men to scout out the Promised Land to see if it was good or bad. Ten of the men came back with what the Bible refers to as "an evil report" (Numbers 13:32). When the twelve scouts returned, they told Moses, "The land is good, but there are giants in it!"

The fear of the giants prevented God's people from entering the land that He had promised to give them. It wasn't really the giants that defeated these people; it was their poor self-image. They only saw the giants; they failed to see God.

Joshua and Caleb were the only ones who had a proper attitude toward the land. They said to Moses and the people, "Let us go up at once and possess it; we are well able to conquer it" (Numbers 13:30). In the end, they were the only ones who were allowed by God to go into the Promised Land.

God had a glorious future planned for all of the Israelites, but all of them did not enter into that future—only the ones who had a proper attitude toward God and toward themselves.

God does not have a bad attitude toward you
—you should not have one toward yourself!

GOD'S WORD FOR YOU

For I know the thoughts and plans that I have for you, says the Lord, thoughts and plans for welfare and peace and not for evil, to give you hope in your final outcome.

JEREMIAH 29:11

God Has a Plan

If you have a poor self-image, it has already adversely affected your past, but you can be healed and not allow the past to repeat itself. Let go of what lies behind, including any negative ways you have felt about yourself, and press on toward the good things God has in store for you.

God has a good plan and a purpose for each of us and a specific way and perfect time to bring it to pass, but not all of us experience it. Many times we live far below the standard that God intends for us to enjoy.

For years I did not exercise my rights and privileges as a child of God. Although I was a Christian and believed I would go to heaven when I died, I did not know that anything could be done about my past, present, or future. I had a poor self-image, and it affected my day-to-day living, as well as my outlook for the future.

Accept God's love for you and make that love the basis for your love and acceptance of yourself. Receive His affirmation, knowing that you are changing and becoming all that He desires you to be. Then start enjoying yourself—where you are—on your way to full spiritual maturity.

Let God be God in your life. Give Him the reins.
He knows what He is doing.

GOD'S WORD FOR YOU

For we are God's [own] handiwork (His workmanship), recreated in Christ Jesus, [born anew] that we may do those good works which God predestined (planned beforehand) for us [taking paths which He prepared ahead of time], that we should walk in them [living the good life which He prearranged and made ready for us to live].

EPHESIANS 2:10

$\mathscr{I}$t's Your Choice!

Rejecting ourselves does not change us. It actually multiplies our problems. Acceptance causes us to face reality and then begin to deal with it. We cannot deal with anything as long as we are refusing to accept it or denying its reality.

God has given us a wonderful gift: *free will.* God is offering us the opportunity to accept ourselves as we are, but we have a free will and can refuse to do so if we so choose. To accept something means to view it as usual, proper, or right.

People who reject themselves do so because they cannot see themselves as proper or right. They only see their flaws and weaknesses, not their beauty and strength. This is an unbalanced attitude probably instilled by authority figures in the past who majored on what was weak and wrong rather than what was strong and right.

In Amos 3:3, we read, "Do two walk together except they make an appointment and have agreed?" To walk with God, we must agree with God. He says He loves us and accepts us; therefore, if we agree with Him, we can no longer hate and reject ourselves.

We need to agree with God that when He created us,
He created something good.

GOD'S WORD FOR YOU

For the Lord corrects and disciplines everyone whom He loves, and He punishes, even scourges, every son whom He accepts and welcomes to His heart and cherishes.

You must submit to and endure [correction] for discipline; God is dealing with you as with sons. For what son is there whom his father does not [thus] train and correct and discipline?

HEBREWS 12:6-7

SELF-ACCEPTANCE ALLOWS CHANGE

Perhaps you have been struggling with accepting yourself. You see the areas in yourself that need to be changed. You desire to be like Jesus. Yet it is very difficult for you to think or say, "I accept myself." You feel that to do so would be to accept all that is wrong with you, but that is not the case.

We cannot even begin the process of change until this issue of self-acceptance is settled in our individual lives. When we truly believe that God loves us unconditionally just as we are, then we will be willing to receive His correction.

Change requires correction—people who do not know they are loved have a very difficult time receiving correction. In order for God to change us, He must correct us. We may hear His correction and even agree with it, but it will only make us feel angry or condemned unless we know it is ultimately going to bring about the change that is needed in our life.

To grow up in God and be changed, we must trust Him. Often He will lead us in ways that we cannot understand, and during those times we must have a tight grip on His love for us.

Be patient with yourself. Keep pressing on and believe that you are changing every day.

GOD'S WORD FOR YOU

Do not be conformed to this world (this age), [fashioned after and adapted to its external, superficial customs], but be transformed (changed) by the [entire] renewal of your mind [by its new ideals and its new attitude], so that you may prove [for yourselves] what is the good and acceptable and perfect will of God, even the thing which is good and acceptable and perfect [in His sight for you].

ROMANS 12:2

"How Can I Change?"

Change does not come through struggle, human effort without God, frustration, self-hatred, self-rejection, guilt, or works of the flesh.

Change in our lives comes as a result of having our minds renewed by the Word of God. As we agree with God and really believe that what He says is true, it gradually begins to manifest itself in us. We begin to think differently, then we begin to talk differently, and finally we begin to act differently. This is a process that develops in stages, and we must always remember that while it is taking place we can still have the attitude, "I'm OK, and I'm on my way!"

Enjoy yourself while you are changing. Enjoy where you are on the way to where you are going. Enjoy the journey! Don't waste all of your "now time" trying to rush into the future. Remember, tomorrow will have troubles of its own (Matthew 6:34).

Relax. Let God be God. Stop being so hard on yourself. Change is a process; it comes little by little.

We can come to Jesus just as we are.
He takes us "as is" and makes
us what we ought to be.

HEALING
FOR DAMAGED
EMOTIONS

Jesus longs to heal our broken hearts
and lavish His great love upon us.

GOD'S WORD FOR YOU

*The Spirit of the Lord God is upon me, because the
Lord has anointed and qualified me to preach the Gospel
of good tidings to the meek, the poor, and afflicted; He
has sent me to bind up and heal the brokenhearted, to
proclaim liberty to the [physical and spiritual] captives and
the opening of the prison and of the eyes to those who are
bound, [Rom. 10:15.]*

*To proclaim the acceptable year of the Lord [the year
of His favor] and the day of vengeance of our God, to
comfort all who mourn, [Matt. 11:2-6; Luke 4:18, 19;
7:22.]*

*To grant [consolation and joy] to those who mourn in
Zion—to give them an ornament (a garland or diadem) of
beauty instead of ashes, the oil of joy instead of mourning,
the garment [expressive] of praise instead of a heavy,
burdened, and failing spirit—that they may be called
oaks of righteousness [lofty, strong, and magnificent,
distinguished for uprightness, justice, and right standing
with God], the planting of the Lord, that He may be
glorified.*

ISAIAH 61:1-3

t w o

HEALING FOR DAMAGED EMOTIONS

motional healing, also referred to as inner healing, is a subject that needs to be talked about in a scriptural, balanced way that produces godly results. Our inner life is much more important than our outer life. The apostle Paul said in 2 Corinthians 4:16 that even though our outer man is progressively decaying and wasting away, our inner self is being progressively renewed day after day. Romans 14:17 lets us know that the Kingdom of God is not meat and drink (not outward things), but it is righteousness, peace, and joy in the Holy Spirit, and Luke 17:21 says the Kingdom of God is within you.

I was sexually, physically, verbally, and emotionally abused from the time I can remember until I finally left home at the age of eighteen. I have been rejected, abandoned, and betrayed. I, too, was an "emotional prisoner" for a long time, but God has healed and transformed me with His love. And He will do the same for you!

In Isaiah 61 the Lord said that He came to heal the brokenhearted. I believe that means those broken inside, those crushed and wounded inwardly. Jesus wants to lead us out of emotional devastation to health and wholeness in the inner man by the power of the Holy Spirit.

Wherever you are spiritually or emotionally,
God will meet you where you are.

GOD'S WORD FOR YOU

And I am convinced and sure of this very thing, that He Who began a good work in you will continue until the day of Jesus Christ [right up to the time of His return], developing [that good work] and perfecting and bringing it to full completion in you.

PHILIPPIANS 1:6-7

ONE STEP AT A TIME

When I speak on the healing of emotional wounds, I like to hold up several different-colored shoestrings tied together in a knot. I tell the audience, "This is you when you first start the process of transformation with God. You're all knotted up. Each knot represents a different problem in your life. Untangling those knots and straightening out those problems is going to take a bit of time and effort, so don't get discouraged if it doesn't happen all at once."

If you want to receive emotional healing and come into an area of wholeness, you must realize that healing is a process. Allow the Lord to deal with you and your problems in His way and in His time. Your part is to cooperate with Him in whatever area He chooses to start dealing with you first.

In our modern, instantaneous society we expect everything to be quick and easy. The Lord never gets in a hurry, and He never quits. Sometimes it may seem that you are not making any progress. That's because the Lord is untying your knots one at a time. The process may be hard and take time, but if you will "stick with the program," sooner or later you will see the victory and experience the freedom you have wanted so long.

God wants you to believe and keep pressing on.

GOD'S WORD FOR YOU

*For we do not have a High Priest Who is unable to
understand and sympathize and have a shared feeling with
our weaknesses and infirmities and liability to the assaults
of temptation, but One Who has been tempted in every
respect as we are, yet without sinning.*

HEBREWS 4:15

Jesus and Emotions

According to the writer of Hebrews, Jesus experienced every emotion and suffered every feeling you and I do, yet without sinning. He did not sin because He did not give in to His wrong feelings. He knew the Word of God in every area of life because He spent years studying it before He began His ministry. You and I will never be able to say no to our feelings if we don't have a strong knowledge of God's Word.

When I am hurt by someone and I feel angry or upset, I pray, "Jesus, I am so glad that You understand what I am feeling right now and that You don't condemn me for feeling this way. I don't want to give vent to my emotions. Help me to forgive those who have wronged me and not slight them, avoid them, or seek to pay them back for the harm they have done me."

God wants us to be more sensitive to the feelings and needs of others and less sensitive to our own feelings and needs. He wants us to deposit ourselves in His hands and let Him take care of us while we are practicing being kind and compassionate and sensitive to other people.

*Make your emotions serve you
—don't spend your life serving them.*

GOD'S WORD FOR YOU

For no temptation (no trial regarded as enticing to sin, no matter how it comes or where it leads) has overtaken you and laid hold on you that is not common to man [that is, no temptation or trial has come to you that is beyond human resistance and that is not adjusted and adapted and belonging to human experience, and such as man can bear]. But God is faithful [to His Word and to His compassionate nature], and He [can be trusted] not to let you be tempted and tried and assayed beyond your ability and strength of resistance and power to endure, but with the temptation He will [always] also provide the way out (the means of escape to a landing place), that you may be capable and strong and powerful to bear up under it patiently.

1 CORINTHIANS 10:13

$\mathcal{N}$o Pain, No Gain!

In moving from devastation to emotional wholeness, even with the Holy Spirit leading us, the pain of the healing process from emotional wounds can be more traumatic than experiencing physical pain. Because I experienced so much emotional pain, I grew weary of hurting. I was attempting to find healing by following the leadership of the Holy Spirit. Yet I could not understand why the process had to be so painful. The Lord showed me how that each time I went through one of the painful events or situations (being sexually abused at home, being ridiculed at school, being subjected to constant fear), it was like a new doorway of pain.

The Lord revealed to me that I had been hiding behind many such "doorways of pain." I was *deep* in bondage, taking refuge behind false personalities, pretenses, and facades. I began to understand that when people are led out of bondage into freedom, they must pass back through similar doorways of pain to get on the other side of those doors. They pass through, not actual experiences such as abuse, but the emotional responses to the experiences. To deliver and heal, the Lord must lead us to face issues, people, and truths that we find difficult, if not impossible, to face on our own.

Remember, God will never allow a temptation to come upon you that you are not able to bear.

GOD'S WORD FOR YOU

There was a certain man there who had suffered with
a deep-seated and lingering disorder for thirty-eight years.
When Jesus noticed him lying there [helpless],
knowing that he had already been a long time in that
condition, He said to him, Do you want to become well?
[Are you really in earnest about getting well?]

JOHN 5:5-6

DO YOU WANT TO GET WELL?

Isn't this an amazing question for Jesus to ask this poor man who had been sick for thirty-eight long years: "Do you really want to become well?" That is the Lord's question to each of us as well.

Do you know there are people who really don't want to get well? They only want to talk about their problem. Are you one of those people? Do you really want to get well, or do you just want to talk about your problem? Sometimes people get addicted to having a problem. It becomes their identity, their life. It defines everything they think and say and do. All their being is centered around that particular problem.

If you have a "deep-seated and lingering disorder," the Lord wants you to know that it does not have to be the central focal point of your entire existence. He wants you to trust Him and cooperate with Him as He leads you to victory over that problem one step at a time.

Whatever our problem may be, God has promised to meet our need and to repay us for our loss. Facing truth is the key to unlocking prison doors that may have held us in bondage.

God yearns to see you become all that
He has planned for you to be.

GOD'S WORD FOR YOU

If you abide in My word [hold fast to My teachings and live in accordance with them], you are truly My disciples.

And you will know the Truth, and the Truth will set you free.

JOHN 8:31-32

Face the Truth

If you are to receive emotional healing and restoration of your broken spirit, you must learn to face the truth. You cannot be set free while living in denial. You cannot pretend either that certain negative events did not happen to you, or that you have not been influenced by them or reacted in response to them.

Many times people who have suffered abuse or some other tragedy in their lives try to act as though it never happened. Early traumatic experiences can cause us to be emotionally damaged and wounded in later life because we develop opinions and attitudes about ourselves based on what we did.

From my own experience, as well as my years of ministry to others, I have come to realize that we human beings are marvelously adept at building walls and cramming things into dark corners, pretending they never happened.

It is so wonderful to have Jesus as a friend, because we don't have to hide anything from Him. He already knows everything about us anyway. We can always come to Him and know we will be loved and accepted no matter what we have suffered or how we have reacted to it.

Even though it may be hard to face the truth,
Jesus promises to be with us and set us free.

GOD'S WORD FOR YOU

But be doers of the Word [obey the message], and not merely listeners to it, betraying yourselves [into deception by reasoning contrary to the Truth].

JAMES 1:22

Listen to and obey My voice, and I will be your God and you will be My people; and walk in the whole way that I command you, that it may be well with you.

JEREMIAH 7:23

OBEY THE WORD

I recall a woman who attended one of my seminars. She desperately wanted to be free of the emotional wounds that had left her insecure and fearful, but nothing seemed to work for her. At the conclusion of the seminar, she told me that she now understood why she had never experienced any progress.

She said, "Joyce, I sat with a group of ladies who had a lot of the same problems that I did. Step by step God had been delivering them. As I listened, I heard them say, 'God led me to do this, and I did it. Then He led me to another thing, and I did it.' I realized that God had also told me to do the same things. The only difference was they did what He said to do, and I didn't."

To receive what God promises us in His Word, we must obey the Word. We must become doers of the Word and not hearers only. Obeying the Word requires consistency and diligence. It can't be hit or miss. We can't just do it for a while to see if it works. There must be a dedication and commitment to do the Word whatever the outcome.

God's way works!
And there is no other way that does.

GOD'S WORD FOR YOU

Confess to one another therefore your faults (your slips, your false steps, your offenses, your sins) and pray [also] for one another, that you may be healed and restored [to a spiritual tone of mind and heart].

JAMES 5:16

Confess Your Faults

I think there is a place for eventually sharing with someone else that which has occurred in our life. There is something tremendously healing about verbalizing it to another person that does wonders for us.

But use wisdom. Be Spirit-led. Choose someone you know you can trust. Be sure that by sharing your burden with someone else, you do not place it upon that individual's shoulders. Also don't go on a digging expedition, trying to dig up old injuries long buried and forgotten.

It is so important to use wisdom and balance in these matters. If you are going to share your problems with someone, let God show you whom to choose as a confidant. Pick a mature believer, someone who is not going to be burdened down or harmed by what you share or use it to hurt you or make you feel worse about yourself.

Many times there is a release that comes to us when we finally tell someone else those secrets that have been crammed in the background of our lives for years, especially when we discover that the person with whom we share them still loves and accepts us in spite of them.

*Bringing things out in the open
causes them to lose their grip on us.*

GOD'S WORD FOR YOU

For I will forgive their iniquity, and I will [seriously] remember their sin no more.

JEREMIAH 31:34

As far as the east is from the west, so far has He removed our transgressions from us.

PSALM 103:12

RECEIVE FORGIVENESS AND FORGET YOUR SIN

No matter what your problem or how bad you feel about yourself as a result of it, God loves you. In Jesus Christ He has given you a new life. He has given you a new family and new friends to love and accept and appreciate and support you. You are okay, and you are going to make it because of the One Who lives on the inside of you and cares for you.

You may have had an abortion, but you need to look in the mirror and confess, "I did that, Lord, and it is a marvel to me to realize that I can stand here and look myself in the eye. But I can do so because I know that even though I did that horrible sin, You have put my sins as far away from me as the east is from the west, and You remember them no more!"

Once we have confessed our sins and asked for God's forgiveness, if we continue to drag them up to Him every time we go to Him in prayer, we are reminding Him of something He has not only *forgiven* but also actually *forgotten.*

God's mercy is new every morning.
Each day we can find a fresh place to begin.

CONFIDENCE

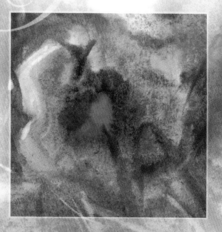

Confidence in Christ is required for us
to truly succeed at being ourselves.

GOD'S WORD FOR YOU

[Most] blessed is the man who believes in, trusts in, and relies on the Lord, and whose hope and confidence the Lord is.

JEREMIAH 17:7

three

CONFIDENCE

o succeed at being ourselves, we must be confident. It is not self-confidence we are to seek, but confidence in Christ. I like *The Amplified Bible* translation of Philippians 4:13, which says, ". . . I am self-sufficient in Christ's sufficiency." It is actually a sin to be confident in ourselves—but to be confident in Christ should be the goal of every believer.

Jesus said, ". . . apart from Me [cut off from vital union with Me] you can do nothing" (John 15:5). We keep attempting to do things in the strength of our own flesh, instead of placing all our confidence in Him.

Most of our internal agony, our struggling and frustration, comes from misplaced confidence. In Philippians 3:3, Paul says that we are to put no confidence in the flesh. This means our own selves as well as our friends and family. I am not saying that we cannot trust anyone, but if we give to others the trust that belongs to God alone, we will not experience victory. God will not allow us to succeed until our confidence is in the right place, or more correctly, in the right Person.

Jesus is the Rock—the only true source of stability. Put your trust in Him.

GOD'S WORD FOR YOU

[God] disarmed the principalities and powers that were ranged against us and made a bold display and public example of them, in triumphing over them in Him and in it [the cross].

COLOSSIANS 2:15

$\mathcal{G}$ET RID OF THE FAILURE SYNDROME

People who have been abused, rejected, or abandoned usually lack confidence. Such individuals are shame-based and guilt-ridden and have a very poor self-image. The devil knows that and begins his assault on personal confidence whenever and wherever he can find an opening. His ultimate goal is total destruction of the person.

The devil knows that an individual without confidence will never step out to do anything edifying for the Kingdom of God or detrimental to Satan's kingdom. He does not want you to fulfill God's plan for your life. If he can make you believe that you are incapable, then you won't even try to accomplish anything worthwhile. Even if you do make an effort, your fear of failure will seal your defeat, which, because of your lack of confidence, you probably expected from the beginning. This is often what is referred to as the "Failure Syndrome."

God wants you to know that the devil is already a defeated foe. Jesus triumphed over him on the cross and made a public display of his disgrace in the spirit realm. Jesus' victory means you can get rid of the failure syndrome. His ability to bring His will to pass in your life is determined by your faith in Him and in His Word.

God's victory purchased on the cross
is total and complete.

GOD'S WORD FOR YOU

Lean on, trust in, and be confident in the Lord with all your heart and mind and do not rely on your own insight or understanding.

In all your ways know, recognize, and acknowledge Him, and He will direct and make straight and plain your paths.

PROVERBS 3:5-6

THE LIE ABOUT SELF-CONFIDENCE

Everyone talks about self-confidence. All kinds of seminars are available on confidence, both in the secular world and the church world. Confidence is generally referred to as "self-confidence" because we all know that we need to feel good about ourselves if we are ever to accomplish anything in life. We have been taught that all people have a basic need to believe in themselves. However, that is not the truth.

Actually, we don't need to believe in ourselves— we need to believe in Jesus in us. We don't dare feel good about ourselves apart from Him.

If we believe the lie of self-confidence, we will create many complicated problems. We will never reach our full potential in Christ; we will live ruled by fear without knowing true joy, fulfillment, or satisfaction, and will lose sight of our right to be an individual. The Holy Spirit will be grieved.

Don't be concerned about yourself, your weaknesses, or your strengths. Get your eyes off of yourself and onto the Lord. If you are weak, He can strengthen you. If you have any strength, it is because He gave it to you. So either way, your eyes should be on Him and not on yourself.

We do not need self-confidence;
we need God-confidence!

GOD'S WORD FOR YOU

Thus says the Lord: Cursed [with great evil] is the strong man who trusts in and relies on frail man, making weak [human] flesh his arm, and whose mind and heart turn aside from the Lord.

JEREMIAH 17:5

$\mathscr{H}$AVE CONFIDENCE IN GOD ALONE

In order to succeed at anything, we must have confidence, but first and foremost it must be confidence in God, not confidence in anything else. We must develop confidence in God's love, goodness, and mercy. We must believe that He wants us to succeed.

God did not create us for failure. We may fail at some things on our way to success, but if we trust Him, He will take even our mistakes and work them out for our good (Romans 8:28).

Hebrews 3:6 tells us we must ". . . hold fast and firm to the end our joyful and exultant confidence and sense of triumph in our hope [in Christ]." It is important to realize that a mistake is not the end of things if we hold on to our confidence.

We all have a destiny, but just because we are destined to do something does not mean that it will automatically happen. I went through many things while God was developing me and my ministry. Often I lost my confidence concerning the call on my life. Each time I had to get my confidence back before I could go forward again.

Put your confidence in God alone, and He will cause you to truly succeed at being yourself.

GOD'S WORD FOR YOU

The man who through faith is just and upright . . .
shall live by faith.

ROMANS 1:17

BE CONSISTENTLY CONFIDENT

Confidence is actually faith in God. We must learn to be consistently confident, not occasionally confident.

I had to learn to remain confident when I was told by friends and family that a woman should not be preaching the Word of God. I knew God had called me to preach His Word, but I was still affected by the rejection of people. I had to grow in confidence to the place where people's opinions and their acceptance or rejection did not affect my confidence level. My confidence had to be in God, not in people.

Romans 1:17 tells us that we can go from faith to faith. I spent many years going from faith to doubt to unbelief and then back to faith. Then I realized that when I lose my confidence, I leave a door open for the devil. If I allow him to steal my confidence, I suddenly have no faith to minister to people.

If you want to succeed, you must be consistently confident. Be confident about your gifts and calling, your ability in Christ. Believe you hear from God and that you are led by the Holy Spirit. Be bold in the Lord. See yourself as a winner in Him!

Don't look to your insecurities; look to God and be confident. He is your strength and salvation.

GOD'S WORD FOR YOU

Yet amid all these things we are more than conquerors and gain a surpassing victory through Him Who loved us.

ROMANS 8:37

More Than Conquerors

We need to have a sense of triumph. Paul assures us that through Christ Jesus we are more than conquerors. Believing that truth gives us confidence.

Sometimes our confidence is shaken when trials come, especially if they are lengthy. We should have so much confidence in God's love for us that no matter what comes against us, we know deep inside that we are more than conquerors. If we are truly confident, we have no need to fear trouble, challenges, or trying times, because we know they will pass.

Whenever a trial of any kind comes against you, always remember: *This too shall pass!* Be confident that during the trial you will learn something that will help you in the future.

Without confidence we are stifled at every turn. Satan drops a bomb, and our dreams are destroyed. Eventually we start over, but we never make much progress. But those who know they are more than conquerors through Jesus Christ make rapid progress.

We must take a step of faith and decide to be confident in all things in Him. Confident people get the job done. They are fulfilled because they are succeeding at being themselves.

We will not succeed at being ourselves
until our confidence is in God.

GOD'S WORD FOR YOU

David was greatly distressed, for the men spoke of stoning him because the souls of them all were bitterly grieved, each man for his sons and daughters. But David encouraged and strengthened himself in the Lord his God.

1 SAMUEL 30:6

THE TORMENT OF SELF-DOUBT

If we don't believe in ourselves, who is going to? God believes in us, and it's a good thing too; otherwise, we might never make any progress. We cannot wait for someone else to come along and encourage us to be all we can be.

When David and his men found themselves in a seemingly hopeless situation, which the men blamed on him, David encouraged and strengthened himself in the Lord. Later on, that situation was totally turned around (1 Samuel 30:1-20).

When David was just a boy, everyone around him discouraged him concerning his ability to fight Goliath. They told him he was too young and too inexperienced, and he didn't have the right armor or the right weapons. But David knew his God and had confidence in Him. David believed that God would be strong in his weakness and give him the victory.

Self-doubt is absolutely tormenting, and we must rid ourselves of it. Like David, we must learn to know our God—about His love, His ways, and His Word— then ultimately we must *decide* whether we believe or not. When we don't doubt ourselves but trust in God, He will give us the victory.

The way to end the torment of self-doubt is to look to God and have faith in His mighty power.

GOD'S WORD FOR YOU

Having gifts (faculties, talents, qualities) that differ according to the grace given us, let us use them: [He whose gift is] prophecy, [let him prophesy] according to the proportion of his faith;

[He whose gift is] practical service, let him give himself to serving; he who teaches, to his teaching;

He who exhorts (encourages), to his exhortation; he who contributes, let him do it in simplicity and liberality; he who gives aid and superintends, with zeal and singleness of mind; he who does acts of mercy, with genuine cheerfulness and joyful eagerness.

ROMANS 12:6-8

The sun is glorious in one way, the moon is glorious in another way, and the stars are glorious in their own [distinctive] way; for one star differs from and surpasses another in its beauty and brilliance.

1 CORINTHIANS 15:41

Confident to Be Different

We are all different. Like the sun, the moon, and the stars, God has created us to be different from one another, and He has done it on purpose. Each of us meets a need, and we are all part of God's overall plan. When we struggle to be like others, we lose ourselves, and we grieve the Holy Spirit. God wants us to fit into His plan, not to feel pressured trying to fit into everyone else's plans. It is all right to be different.

We are all born with different temperaments, different physical features, different fingerprints, different gifts and abilities. Our goal should be to find out what we individually are supposed to be, and then succeed at being that.

Romans 12 teaches us to give ourselves to our gift. We are to find out what we are good at and then throw ourselves wholeheartedly into it.

We should be free to love and accept ourselves and one another without feeling pressure to compare or compete. Secure people who know God loves them and has a plan for them are not threatened by the abilities of others. They enjoy what other people can do, and they enjoy what they can do.

God gave you gifts and wants you to focus on your potential instead of your limitations.

GOD'S WORD FOR YOU

Whoever finds his [lower] life will lose it [the higher life], and whoever loses his [lower] life on My account will find it [the higher life].

MATTHEW 10:39

Don't Lose Yourself

How can we succeed at being ourselves if we don't know ourselves? Life is like a maze sometimes, and it is easy to get lost. Everyone, it seems, expects something different from us. There is pressure coming at us from every direction to keep others happy and meet their needs.

We then attempt to become what they want us to be. In the process, we may lose ourselves. We may fail to discover what God's intention is for us. We try so hard to please everyone else and yet not be pleased ourselves.

For years I tried to be so many things that I wasn't that I got myself totally confused. I had to get off the merry-go-round and ask myself: "Who am I living for? Why am I doing all these things? Have I become a people-pleaser? Am I really in God's will for my life?"

Have you also lost yourself? Are you frustrated from trying to meet all the demands of other people while feeling unfulfilled yourself? You need to take a stand and be determined to know your identity, your direction, and your calling—God's will for your life. You will find yourself by finding His will for your life and doing it.

If you give your heart to doing His will,
you'll find your true self.

DEVELOP
YOUR
POTENTIAL

*We are free to develop our potential
because of what God has done
through Christ for us!*

GOD'S WORD FOR YOU

Do you not know that in a race all the runners compete, but [only] one receives the prize? So run [your race] that you may lay hold [of the prize] and make it yours.

1 CORINTHIANS 9:24

four

DEVELOP YOUR POTENTIAL

When we are confident and free from tormenting fears and self-doubt, we are able to develop our potential and succeed at being all God intended us to be. But we cannot develop our potential if we fear failure. We will be so afraid of failing or making mistakes that it will prevent us from stepping out.

I often see people who have great potential, and yet when opportunities and promotions are offered them, they quickly turn them down. In many cases, they are insecure and unaware of how much they could accomplish for the Kingdom of God if they would only step out in faith and confidence.

When we are insecure, frequently we will stay with what is safe and familiar rather than taking a chance on stepping out and failing. We avoid accepting greater responsibility, and the truth is that none of us is ever ready. But when God is ready to move in our lives, we need to believe that He will equip us with what we need at the time we need it.

Humbly leaning on God leads to success. If our confidence is in Christ rather than ourselves, we are free to develop our potential, because we are free from the fear of failure.

*The development and manifestation of potential
requires firm faith, not wishful thinking.*

GOD'S WORD FOR YOU

Any enterprise is built by wise planning, becomes strong through common sense, and profits wonderfully by keeping abreast of the facts.

PROVERBS 24:3-4 TLB

Don't Make Small Plans!

I hope you have a dream or a vision in your heart for something greater than what you have now. It is important to have dreams and visions for our lives. We atrophy without something to reach for. God has created us to have goals. Ephesians 3:20 KJV tells us that God is "able to do exceedingly abundantly above all we can ask or think." We need to think big thoughts, hope for big things, and ask for big things.

Quite often we look at a task and think there is no way we can do what needs to be done. That happens because we look at ourselves when we should be looking at God.

When the Lord called Joshua to take the place of Moses and lead the Israelites into the Promised Land, He said to him, "As I was with Moses, so I will be with you; I will not fail you or forsake you" (Joshua 1:5).

If God promises to be with us—and He does— that is really all we need. His strength is made perfect in our weakness (2 Corinthians 12:9 KJV). Whatever ingredients we are lacking in the natural man, He adds to the spiritual man.

God is honored when we believe Him to do the "big things" we have dreamed about.

GOD'S WORD FOR YOU

. . . be strong in the Lord [be empowered through your union with Him]; draw your strength from Him [that strength which His boundless might provides].

EPHESIANS 6:10

. . . they that wait upon the Lord shall renew their strength; they shall mount up with wings as eagles; they shall run, and not be weary; and they shall walk, and not faint.

ISAIAH 40:31 KJV

76

DRAW UPON THE STRENGTH OF THE LORD

When God called me into ministry, I wanted to fulfill His call more than anything. I didn't even know where to begin, let alone how to finish the task. As God gave me anointed ideas and opened to me doors of opportunity for service, I stepped out in faith. Each time He met me with the strength, wisdom, and ability that was needed to be successful.

If you're going to learn to be successful in the task that God sets before you, you have to learn the secret of drawing on His strength. Your strength will run out, but His never will.

In Ephesians 6:10, Paul assures us that the Holy Spirit will pour strength into our human spirit as we fellowship with Him. And the prophet Isaiah says that those who have learned the secret of waiting on the Lord "shall mount up with wings as eagles" (Isaiah 40:31). It is very obvious from these scriptures that we are strengthened as we go to God for what we are lacking.

Everything we are and need is found "in Christ." In Him we are redeemed. In Him we are complete. Our wisdom, strength, peace, and hope are in Him. Our everything is in Him!

God does not just want to give you strength
—He wants to be your strength.

GOD'S WORD FOR YOU

. . . let us strip off and throw aside every encumbrance (unnecessary weight) and that sin which so readily (deftly and cleverly) clings to and entangles us, and let us run with patient endurance and steady and active persistence the appointed course of the race that is set before us.

HEBREWS 12:1

RUNNING THE RACE

When the writer of the letter to the Hebrews told them to *strip off and throw aside every encumbrance*, he was thinking of the runners in his day who entered races with the intention of winning. They literally stripped off their clothes down to a simple loincloth. They made sure nothing could entangle them and prevent them from running their fastest. They were running to win!

To develop our potential and succeed at becoming all that God intended us to be, we must take an inventory of our life and prune off anything that entangles us or simply steals our time. Hebrews 12:1 tells us to strip off and throw aside every encumbrance and the *sin* that entangles us. It is virtually impossible to be a spiritual success with known, willful sin in our lives. We must have an aggressive attitude about keeping sin out of our lives.

When God says something is wrong, then it is wrong. We don't need to discuss, theorize, blame, make excuses, or feel sorry for ourselves—we need to agree with God, ask for forgiveness, and obey the Holy Spirit to get that sin out of our lives forever.

Lay aside everything that hinders
and run the race of holiness.
The reward is God Himself!

GOD'S WORD FOR YOU

Do you not know that in a race all the runners compete, but [only] one receives the prize? So run [your race] that you may lay hold [of the prize] and make it yours.

Now every athlete who goes into training conducts himself temperately and restricts himself in all things. They do it to win a wreath that will soon wither, but we [do it to receive a crown of eternal blessedness] that cannot wither.

Therefore I do not run uncertainly (without definite aim). I do not box like one beating the air and striking without an adversary.

But [like a boxer] I buffet my body [handle it roughly, discipline it by hardships] and subdue it, for fear that after proclaiming to others the Gospel and things pertaining to it, I myself should become unfit [not stand the test, be unapproved and rejected as a counterfeit].

1 CORINTHIANS 9:24-27

BE TEMPERATE IN ALL THINGS

Those of us who intend to run the race to win must conduct ourselves temperately and restrict ourselves in all things. We cannot expect someone else to make us do what is right. We must listen to the Holy Spirit and take action ourselves.

Paul said he buffeted his body. Paul was running the race to win! He knew he could not develop his potential without bringing his body, mind, and emotions under control.

Self-discipline is the most important feature in any life, especially in the life of the Christian. Unless we discipline our minds, our mouths, and our emotions, we will live in ruin. One major emotion many need to learn to rule is their temper.

We can never achieve our full potential if our flesh is controlling our emotions. If we are truly intent on running the race, we must resist negative emotions. There are many negative emotions other than just anger, and we must be ready to take authority over them as soon as they rear their ugly heads.

We must allow the Holy Spirit to replace all those destructive emotions with His fruit: "love, joy, peace, patience, kindness, goodness, faithfulness, gentleness, self-control" (Galatians 5:22-23 NASB).

*Self-improvement does not come through self-effort;
it comes from dependence upon the Holy Spirit.*

GOD'S WORD FOR YOU

For who has known the mind of the Lord and who has understood His thoughts, or who has [ever] been His counselor? [Isa. 40:13, 14.]

ROMANS 11:34

GOD'S WAY IS BETTER

We need to come to the realization that God is smarter than we are. No matter what you or I may think, God's way is better than ours. We often think we know what's best, and then we throw all our flesh into bringing it to pass.

Often we experience a lot of disappointment, which hinders joy and enjoyment, due to deciding for ourselves that something has to be done a certain way or by a certain time. When we want something very strongly, we can easily convince ourselves that it is God's will.

God has no need of a counselor to tell Him what He should do for us. His will is perfect, and He has good plans for us to become all that He intends us to be. The prophet Jeremiah says, "For I know the thoughts and plans that I have for you, says the Lord, thoughts and plans for welfare and peace and not for evil, to give you hope in your final outcome" (Jeremiah 29:11).

When we face puzzling situations, we should say, "Well, Lord, this does not make any sense to me right now, but I trust You. I believe You love me and that You are doing what is best for me."

God does not need our counsel in order to work;
He needs our faith.

GOD'S WORD FOR YOU

My brethren, count it all joy when you fall into various trials, knowing that the testing of your faith produces patience. But let patience have its perfect work, that you may be perfect and complete, lacking nothing.

JAMES 1:2-4 NKJV

And let us not be weary in well doing: for in due season we shall reap, if we faint not.

GALATIANS 6:9 KJV

WAIT ON GOD'S PERFECT TIMING

As God is working out His perfect plan for us, we often want it to happen right now. But character development takes time and patience.

James tells us that when patience has had its perfect work, we will be perfect (fully developed) and complete, lacking nothing. It also speaks about trials of all kinds, and it is during these trials that we are instructed to be patient. Patience is not the ability to wait. It is the ability to keep a good attitude while waiting. Patience is a fruit of the Spirit that manifests itself in a calm, positive attitude despite the circumstances.

"Due season" is God's season, not ours. We are in a hurry, but God isn't. He takes time to do things right—He lays a solid foundation before He attempts to build a building. We are God's building under construction. He is the Master Builder, and He knows what He is doing. God's timing seems to be His own little secret. The Bible promises us that He will never be late, but I have also discovered that He is usually not early. It seems that He takes every available opportunity to develop the fruit of patience in us.

Our potential is only developed
as our patience is developed.

GOD'S WORD FOR YOU

*Are you so foolish and so senseless and so silly?
Having begun [your new life spiritually] with the [Holy]
Spirit, are you now reaching perfection [by dependence]
on the flesh?*

*Have you suffered so many things and experienced so
much all for nothing (to no purpose)—if it really is to no
purpose and in vain?*

*Then does He Who supplies you with His marvelous
[Holy] Spirit and works powerfully and miraculously
among you do so on [the grounds of your doing] what the
Law demands, or because of your believing in and
adhering to and trusting in and relying on the message that
you heard?*

GALATIANS 3:3-5

BEGUN BY FAITH, FINISHED BY FAITH

We need to ask ourselves what Paul was asking the "foolish," "senseless," and "silly" Galatians: Having begun our new lives in Christ by dependence on the Spirit, are we now trying to live them in the flesh?

Just as we are saved by grace (God's unmerited favor) through faith, and not by works of the flesh (Ephesians 2:8-9), so we need to learn to live by grace through faith, and not by works of the flesh.

When we were saved, we were in no condition to help ourselves. What kind of condition are we in now that we have been saved by grace through faith in the finished work of Jesus Christ? We still are in no condition to help ourselves. We have to completely run out of trying to make this new life work by our own effort. Until we are thoroughly convinced we can't do it, we will be doing what the foolish Galatians were trying to do: *live the new life by effort in the flesh.*

The flesh profits us nothing. Only the Spirit can cause us to grow up into the perfection of Christ.

*It is the power of the Holy Spirit
that enables us to live this new life.*

GOD'S WORD FOR YOU

And all of us, as with unveiled face, [because we]
continued to behold [in the Word of God] as in a mirror
the glory of the Lord, are constantly being transfigured
into His very own image in ever increasing splendor and
from one degree of glory to another; [for this comes] from
the Lord [Who is] the Spirit.

2 CORINTHIANS 3:18

From Glory to Glory

How do you see yourself?

Are you able to honestly evaluate yourself and your behavior and not come under condemnation? Are you able to look at how far you still have to go, but also at how far you have come? Where you are now is not where you will end up. Have a vision for the finish line, or you will never get out of the starting block.

In 2 Corinthians 3:18, Paul states that God changes us "from one degree of glory to another." In other words, the changes in us personally, as well as those in our circumstances, take place in degrees.

You are in a glory right now!

If you are born again, then you are somewhere on the path of the righteous. You may not be as far along as you would like to be, but thank God you are on the path. You now belong to the household of God and are being transformed by Him day by day. Enjoy the glory you are in right now and don't get jealous of where others may be. I don't believe we pass into the next degree of glory until we have learned to enjoy the one we are in at the moment.

Don't be too hard on yourself. God is changing you day by day as you trust Him.

EXPERIENCING
THE LOVE
OF GOD

*God's love for you is the foundation
for your faith, for your freedom
from sin, and for your ability
to minister to others without fear.*

GOD'S WORD FOR YOU

In this the love of God was made manifest (displayed) where we are concerned: in that God sent His Son, the only begotten or unique [Son], into the world so that we might live through Him.

1 JOHN 4:9

five

EXPERIENCING
THE LOVE OF GOD

ave you ever asked yourself, "Am I lovable?" You may have immediately said, "No, I'm not!"

I thought I was unlovable before I came to understand the true nature of God's love and His reason for loving me. I was impatient with people, legalistic and harsh, judgmental, rude, selfish, and unforgiving. A breakthrough came in my life when God began to show me that I could not love others because I had never received His love for me. I acknowledged the Bible teaching that God loved me, but it was not a reality in my heart.

God can love us because He wants to; it pleases Him. Just as it is impossible for God not to love, so it is impossible for us to do anything to keep Him from loving us. Once you realize that you are loved by God, not because of anything you are or anything you have done, then you can quit trying to deserve His love or earn His love and simply receive it and enjoy it.

Once your heart is filled with the knowledge of God's awesome unconditional love, you can begin to love Him in return: *We love Him, because He first loved us.*

Knowing that God loves you gives you confidence in Him and trust in His faithfulness.

GOD'S WORD FOR YOU

For [if we are] in Christ Jesus, neither circumcision nor uncircumcision counts for anything, but only faith activated and energized and expressed and working through love.

GALATIANS 5:6

Love, Trust, and Faith

Stop trying so hard to get faith and please God, and start spending all that time and effort with God, loving Him. We are only going to be able to walk in faith based on what we believe about our relationship with God.

Galatians 5:6 says that faith works by love. Faith will not work without love. Everybody thinks that this scripture means that if they don't love other people, their faith won't work. What it means is that if they don't know how much God loves them, their faith won't work.

Trusting God and walking in faith is leaning on Him and trusting Him for everything. You can't do that with someone if you don't know he loves you. You have the love of God inside you, and all you need is to begin to recognize it when He shows you. The Bible says, "We love Him, because He first loved us" (1 John 4:19). It would be impossible for you to love God if you weren't assured of the fact that He loved you first.

It is all down inside you, in your heart. God loves you! You are wonderful! You are precious! Nobody in all the world will ever love you as God loves you.

Faith works by letting God love you.

GOD'S WORD FOR YOU

In this is love: not that we loved God, but that He loved us and sent His Son to be the propitiation (the atoning sacrifice) for our sins.

1 JOHN 4:10

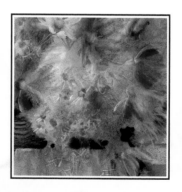

God's Love Will Change You

Meditate on God's love for you. That's what is going to change you. If you don't like something about yourself, *"knowing that you know"* that God loves you is going to change it.

God wants you to spend time with Him in fellowship and worship on a daily basis. That's what will change you. It is the private time you spend with God, just loving Him and letting Him love you, that is going to cause you to grow up and be strong in your spirit.

The devil will give you one excuse after another for not spending time with God. Get serious with God and cry out to Him. *The Word of God and fellowship with Him will change you.* Paul says in Philippians 4:13, "I can do all things through Christ which strengtheneth me" (KJV). In other words, there is nothing in all creation you can't do through the power of Jesus Christ.

Use the problems that come against you as opportunities to grow. Find out what God will do because He loves you! If you will lean on God and let God love you and you love Him, you can forget all the trying to operate in faith and enter into rest.

All blessings will come through letting God love you.

GOD'S WORD FOR YOU

But God shows and clearly proves His [own] love for us by the fact that while we were still sinners, Christ (the Messiah, the Anointed One) died for us.

ROMANS 5:8

*L*OVE IS UNCONDITIONAL

According to God's Word, He loved us before the world was formed, before we loved Him or believed in Him or had ever done anything either good or evil.

God does not require us to earn His love, and we must not require others to earn ours. We must realize that love is something we are to become. It is not something we do and then don't do. We cannot turn it on and off, depending on who we want to give it to and how they are treating us.

As believers in Jesus Christ, the love we are to manifest to the world is the unconditional *love of God* flowing through us to them. We cannot understand this God-kind of love with our minds. It far surpasses mere knowledge. It is a revelation that God gives to His children by the Holy Spirit.

Unconditional love thinks long range. It sees what people can become if only someone will love them. That is what God did for us. He looked long range and saw that His unconditional love could conform us to the image of His Son.

Receive God's mercy and love; you cannot
give away something you do not have.

GOD'S WORD FOR YOU

Do not let yourself be overcome by evil, but overcome (master) evil with good.

ROMANS 12:21

GOD'S LOVE OVERCOMES AND TRANSFORMS

A mean, evil individual can be completely transformed by regular, persistent doses of God's love. Because people's religious experiences in many cases have been unfulfilling to them, they have never entered into a relationship with Jesus Christ that is personal enough for them to begin receiving His healing, transforming love.

Religion often gives people rules to follow and laws to keep. It leads them to believe they must earn God's love and favor through good works. That is the exact opposite of true biblical teaching.

God's Word says that "mercy triumphs over judgment" (James 2:13 NKJV). God's goodness leads men to repentance (Romans 2:4), not the keeping of laws and rules. Jesus did not come to give man religion. He came to give man a deep personal love relationship with the Father through Him.

God's unconditional love does not allow people to remain the same; instead, it loves them while they are changing. Jesus said that He did not come for the well, but for the sick (Matthew 9:12). Our world today is sick, and there is no answer for what ails it except Jesus Christ and all that He stands for.

*Unconditional love will overcome evil
and transform lives.*

GOD'S WORD FOR YOU

Love bears up under anything and everything that comes, is ever ready to believe the best of every person, its hopes are fadeless under all circumstances, and it endures everything [without weakening].

Love never fails [never fades out or becomes obsolete or comes to an end].

1 CORINTHIANS 13:7-8

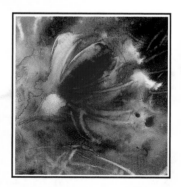

$\mathscr{L}$OVE NEVER FAILS

The God-kind of love bears up under anything and everything that comes. It endures everything without weakening. It is determined not to give up on even the hardest case. The hard-core individual who persists in being rebellious can be eventually melted by love. The Bible says, "While we were yet in weakness [powerless to help ourselves], at the fitting time Christ died for (in behalf of) the ungodly" (Romans 5:6).

It is hard to keep showing love to someone who never seems to appreciate it or even respond to it. It is difficult to keep showing love to those individuals who take from us all we are willing to give, but who never give anything back.

We are not responsible for how others act, only how we act. We have experienced the love of God by His mercy, and now He commands us to show that same kind of love to the world. Our reward does not come from man, but from God. Even when our good deeds seem to go unnoticed, God notices and promises to reward us openly for them: ". . . your deeds of charity may be in secret; and your Father Who sees in secret will reward you openly" (Matthew 6:4).

God is love, and love never quits.

GOD'S WORD FOR YOU

For out of His fullness (abundance) we have all received [all had a share and we were all supplied with] one grace after another and spiritual blessing upon spiritual blessing and even favor upon favor and gift [heaped] upon gift.

JOHN 1:16

BELIEVE AND RECEIVE GOD'S LOVE

Again and again, the Bible speaks of receiving from God. He is always pouring out His blessing, and we should, as empty, thirsty vessels, learn to take in freely all that He offers us.

In the spiritual realm, when you and I believe something, we receive it into our heart. In the world, we are taught to believe what we see. In God's Kingdom, we must learn to believe first, and then we will see manifested what we have believed (received, admitted in our heart).

When Jesus said that whatever we ask of God, believing, will be *granted* to us, He was saying that we will receive it *free*.

One of our biggest challenges is that we do not trust the word "free." We quickly find out in the world's system that things really are not free. Even when we are told they are free, there is usually a hidden cost somewhere.

But God's Kingdom of grace and love is not like the world's. God's wondrous love is a gift He freely gives us. All we need to do is open our hearts, believe His Word, and receive it with thankfulness.

Believe that God loves you with an everlasting love.

GOD'S WORD FOR YOU

And we know (understand, recognize, are conscious of, by observation and by experience) and believe (adhere to and put faith in and rely on) the love God cherishes for us. God is love, and he who dwells and continues in love dwells and continues in God, and God dwells and continues in him.

1 JOHN 4:16

UNDERSTAND GOD'S LOVE

First John 4:16 is a key scripture for me because it says that *we should be conscious and aware of God's love and put faith in it.* I was unconscious and unaware of God's love for a long time; therefore, I was not putting faith in His love for me.

When the Holy Spirit convicted me, I did not know how to say, "Yes, I made a mistake," then go to God, ask for His forgiveness, receive His love, and press on. Instead, I would spend hours and even days feeling guilty about each little thing I did wrong. I was literally tormented! John tells us that fear has torment, but that the perfect love of God casts out fear (1 John 4:18). God's love for me was perfect because it was based on Him, not on me. So even when I failed, He kept loving me.

God's love for you is perfect. When you fail, do you stop receiving God's love and start punishing yourself by feeling guilty and condemned? Don't listen to the devil's lie. Understand and believe God's intense love for you. Don't carry the enemy's burden of guilt. Believe and receive God's yoke of love.

God intends to love us.
He has to love us—He is love!

GOD'S WORD FOR YOU

. . . you are living the life of the Spirit, if the [Holy]
Spirit of God [really] dwells within you [directs and
controls you].

ROMANS 8:9

$\mathscr{L}$ET LOVE TAKE CHARGE

When love takes charge of us (which is another way of saying, when God takes charge of us), we cannot think bad things about people. We don't even want to.

We are not really living the life of the Spirit until we allow the Holy Spirit to control every area of our life. He will certainly never get control of our life until He has control of our thoughts and words.

Being led by the Spirit is central to a victorious Christian life. As long as we think our own thoughts and speak our own words, we will never experience victory.

Our life is a reflection of our thoughts. It is impossible to have a good life unless we have trained ourselves to have good thoughts. If we want others to see Jesus reflected in our life, then His mind must be reflected in us. We must be led by the Spirit in our thinking; that is where all Spirit-led living begins.

Be determined to love God, yourself, and others with your thoughts. Let God's love take charge in your life.

We can let the mind of the flesh control us, or we can choose the Holy Spirit and His way of thinking.

LOVING OTHERS

Love is a divine circle.
First, God loves us, and by faith
we receive His love. We then love
ourselves in a balanced way. We give
love back to God, and then we
learn to love other people.

GOD'S WORD FOR YOU

*By this shall all [men] know that you are My disciples,
if you love one another [if you keep on showing love
among yourselves].*

JOHN 13:35

six

LOVING OTHERS

t took me about forty-five years to realize that love was not the main focus in my life. We need to show the world Jesus. We do that by walking in His love.

Jesus Himself taught on love and walked in love. The world is looking for love, and God is love (1 John 4:8). God wants Christians who are committed to developing the character of Jesus Christ in their own lives and then go out as Christ's ambassadors (2 Corinthians 5:20).

To be His ambassadors, we must have our minds renewed to what love really is. Love is not a feeling we have; it is a decision to treat people the way Jesus would treat them.

When we truly commit to walk in love, it usually causes a huge shift in our lifestyle. Many of our ways—our thoughts, our conversation, our habits—have to change. Love is tangible; it is evident to everyone who comes in contact with it.

Loving others does not come easily or without personal sacrifice. Each time we choose to love someone, it will cost us something—time, money, or effort. That's why we are told to count the cost before we make the commitment (Luke 14:25-33).

Loving others does not depend on our feelings;
it's a choice me make.

GOD'S WORD FOR YOU

They tie up heavy loads, hard to bear, and place them on men's shoulders, but they themselves will not lift a finger to help bear them.

MATTHEW 23:4

Take the Pressure Off Other People

You and I pressure ourselves and other people when we have unrealistic expectations. God does not want us to live under this kind of pressure.

We can expect more out of people than they are able to give us. Continued pressure on people we are in relationship with will ultimately cause the collapse of that relationship. *All people everywhere are looking for love and acceptance.*

I remember the years I furiously tried to change my husband, Dave, and each of our children in different ways. Those were frustrating years, because no matter what I tried, it didn't work!

As humans, all of us require space, or freedom, to be who we are. We want to be accepted as we are. We don't want people giving us the message, even subtly, that we must change in order to be "in."

I am not saying that we must accept sin in other people and merely put up with it. I am saying that *the way to change is prayer, not pressure!* If we love people and pray for them, God will work.

For change to last, it must come from the inside out. Only God can cause that type of heart change.

❦

We cannot change people by pressuring them or by nagging them. Only prayer and God's love will work.

GOD'S WORD FOR YOU

But if anyone has this world's goods (resources for sustaining life) and sees his brother and fellow believer in need, yet closes his heart of compassion against him, how can the love of God live and remain in him?

Little children, let us not love [merely] in theory or in speech but in deed and in truth (in practice and in sincerity).

1 JOHN 3:17-18

Loving With Material Goods

Many people love things and use people to get them. God intends for us to love people and use things to bless them. Sharing our possessions with others is one way to move love from the "talking-about-it stage" to the "doing-it stage."

God has given us a heart of compassion, but by our own choice we open or close it. As believers in Jesus Christ, God gives us His Spirit and puts a new heart in us. Ezekiel 11:19 says that this new heart is sensitive to God's touch. Something deep in every believer wants to help others. However, selfishness can make us so aggressive about our own desires that we become oblivious to the needs around us.

People are hurting everywhere. Some are poor; others are sick or lonely. Still others are emotionally wounded or have spiritual needs. A simple act of kindness to an insecure person can make that individual feel loved and valuable.

People can get caught in the trap of striving to have more. The struggle often produces little or no results. We should strive to excel in giving to others. If we do so, we will find that God makes sure we have enough to meet our own needs plus plenty to give away.

*There is no greater blessing
than giving to others in need.*

GOD'S WORD FOR YOU

As it is written, He [the benevolent person] scatters abroad; He gives to the poor; His deeds of justice and goodness and kindness and benevolence will go on and endure forever!

2 CORINTHIANS 9:9

Everyone Needs a Blessing

It is both good and scriptural to bless the poor. They should be one of our primary targets.

Look for people who are needy and bless them. Share what you have with those who are less fortunate than you are. But remember, everyone needs a blessing—even the rich, the successful, and those who appear to have everything.

We all need to be encouraged, edified, complimented, and appreciated. We all get weary at times and need other people to say to us, "I just wanted to let you know that I appreciate you and all you do."

I believe God blesses us so we can be a blessing —not only in a few places, but everywhere we go! So remember to sow into the poor and the rich, the downtrodden and the successful (2 Corinthians 9:6-7).

If you live to meet needs and to bring others joy, you will find "joy unspeakable" in the process (1 Peter 1:8 KJV).

I want to leave something as a result of my journey through life. I refuse to pass through it as a "taker." I have decided to be a "giver." I want to bless people in tangible ways. I pray that you have the same desire.

Start using what you have to be a blessing, and your well will never run dry.

GOD'S WORD FOR YOU

Love one another with brotherly affection [as members of one family], giving precedence and showing honor to one another.

ROMANS 12:10

*L*OVE GIVES PREFERENCE TO OTHERS

Giving preference to others requires a willingness to adapt and adjust. It means to allow others to go first or to have the best of something. Each time we show preference, we have to make a mental adjustment. We were planning to be first, but we decide to be second. We are in a hurry, but we decide to wait on someone else who seems to have a greater need.

A person is not yet rooted and grounded in love until he or she has learned to show preference to others (Ephesians 3:17 NKJV). Anyone who wants to be a leader in the Kingdom of God must be willing to be a servant (Matthew 23:11).

We have multiple opportunities to adapt and adjust almost every day. If we are locked into our plans, we will have a difficult time doing so. Don't just learn to adjust, but learn to do it with a good attitude. Learning to do these things is learning to walk in love and humility.

Jesus humbled Himself and came to the earth as the Son of Man to save us. We cannot show preference and help others unless we are willing to follow His example and humble ourselves.

Only the Holy Spirit can change us from proud individuals into humble servants of God and man.

GOD'S WORD FOR YOU

*And Peter opened his mouth and said: Most certainly
and thoroughly I now perceive and understand that God
shows no partiality and is no respecter of persons.*

ACTS 10:34

Love Is Impartial

If love is unconditional, then it must not show partiality.

This does not mean that we cannot have special friends or that we cannot be more involved with certain people. It means that we cannot treat some people one way and other people a different way. Our love is not unconditional if we are only kind to those with whom we are good friends, and not care how we treat those who are of no interest or importance to us.

God has given me several special friends in my life who are "in the same flow" as I am. But He has also taught me to treat everyone with respect, to make them feel valued, to listen to them when they are talking to me and not to judge them in a critical way.

Our love walk can readily be seen by how we treat people who cannot do us any good, people with whom we are not interested in developing a relationship. Loving others frequently requires sacrifice. It requires that we put others first, doing what benefits them, and not just us.

The Word of God tells us that He does not show partiality, that He is no respecter of persons. As His representatives, we also are not to show partiality or practice favoritism.

Let God show you how to love everyone without partiality.

GOD'S WORD FOR YOU

For you, brethren, were [indeed] called to freedom; only [do not let your] freedom be an incentive to your flesh and an opportunity or excuse [for selfishness], but through love you should serve one another.

For the whole Law [concerning human relationships] is complied with in the one precept, You shall love your neighbor as [you do] yourself.

GALATIANS 5:13-14

$\mathscr{F}$REE TO BE SERVANTS

Jesus said, in essence, "If you love Me, you will obey Me" (John 14:21). To say "I love Jesus" and walk in disobedience is deception. Words are wonderful, but a full love walk must be much more than words.

I definitely love my husband, but the fulfillment of love must find some service to flow through. How can I say I love my husband if I never want to do anything for him? It is very easy to slide into the worldly flow of "everybody wait on me," but I am determined to swim upstream, against the pull of my flesh, and to be a servant and a blessing everywhere I go.

Jesus instructed His disciples to feed the hungry, give water to the thirsty, clothe the naked, care for the sick, and visit those in prison (Matthew 25:34-45). Jesus makes it very plain that if we have done nothing kind for others, then we have done nothing for Him.

Serving others sets them free to love. It disarms even the most hateful individual. The whole purpose in being a servant is to show others the love of God that He has shown us so that they too can share in it—and then pass it on.

When we serve others in love, God will reward us with a sense of His manifest Presence.

GOD'S WORD FOR YOU

For though we walk (live) in the flesh, we are not carrying on our warfare according to the flesh and using mere human weapons.

For the weapons of our warfare are not physical [weapons of flesh and blood], but they are mighty before God for the overthrow and destruction of strongholds,

[Inasmuch as we] refute arguments and theories and reasonings and every proud and lofty thing that sets itself up against the [true] knowledge of God; and we lead every thought and purpose away captive into the obedience of Christ (the Messiah, the Anointed One).

2 CORINTHIANS 10:3-5

Don't Let Selfishness Win the War

We are definitely in a war. The Bible teaches us that the weapons of our warfare are not carnal, natural weapons, but ones that are mighty through God for the pulling down of strongholds. The stronghold of love grown cold must be pulled down in our lives.

I believe Satan has launched high-tech spiritual warfare against the church, using humanism, materialism, and widespread selfishness as his bait. We must win the war against these things, and the only way to combat them is with a strong love walk.

Purposely forgetting about ourselves and our problems and doing something for someone else while we are hurting is one of the most powerful things we can do to overcome evil.

When Jesus was on the cross in intense suffering, He took time to comfort the thief next to Him (Luke 23:39-43). When Stephen was being stoned, he prayed for those stoning him, asking God not to lay the sin to their charge (Acts 7:59-60).

If the church of Jesus Christ, His body here on earth, will wage war against selfishness and walk in love, the world will begin to take notice.

Walking in love is spiritual warfare.

GOD'S WORD FOR YOU

And let us consider and give attentive, continuous care to watching over one another, studying how we may stir up (stimulate and incite) to love and helpful deeds and noble activities.

HEBREWS 10:24

Pleasant words are as a honeycomb, sweet to the mind and healing to the body.

PROVERBS 16:24

Develop the Habit of Love

If we intend to develop the habit of love, then we must develop the habit of loving people with our words. Multitudes of people need someone to believe in them. They have been wounded by wrong words, but right words can bring healing in their lives.

The fleshly (lower, sensual) nature points out flaws, weaknesses, and failures. It seems to feed on the negatives in life. It sees and magnifies all that is wrong with people and situations. But the Bible says in Romans 12:21 that we are to overcome evil with good.

Walking in the Spirit (continually following the prompting or leading, guiding, and working of the Holy Spirit through our own spirit instead of being led by our emotions) requires being positive. God is positive, and in order to walk with Him, we must agree with Him (Amos 3:3).

It is easy to find something wrong with everyone, but love covers a multitude of sins: "Above all things have intense and unfailing love for one another, for love covers a multitude of sins [forgives and disregards the offenses of others]" (1 Peter 4:8).

Believing the best of people and speaking words
that build them up is one way of loving them.

THE POWER OF
DETERMINATION

I WILL
NOT QUIT

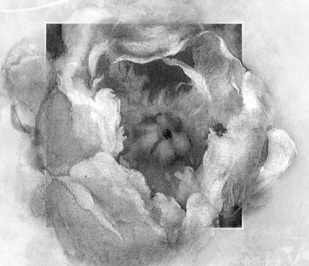

*If you will obey God and never give in or
give up, then nothing — no person on earth,
no devil in hell, no inability you have,
nothing from your past — will be able
to keep you from being successful.*

GOD'S WORD FOR YOU

*For this commandment which I command you this day
is not too difficult for you, nor is it far off.*

DEUTERONOMY 30:11

one

I WILL NOT QUIT

o often, someone will come to me for advice and prayer, and when I tell them what the Word of God says, or what I think the Holy Spirit is saying, their response is, "I know that's right; God has been showing me the same thing. But, Joyce, it's just too hard." It is one of the most commonly expressed excuses I hear from people.

When I initially began to see from the Word of God how I was supposed to live and behave, and compared it to where I was, I also said, "I want to do things Your way, God, but it is so hard." God graciously showed me this is a lie the enemy tries to inject into our minds to get us to give up. God's commandments are not too difficult or too far away.

Walking in obedience to God is not too difficult because He has given His Spirit to work in us powerfully and to help us in all He has asked of us (John 14:16). He is in us and with us all the time to enable us to do what we cannot do, and to do with ease what would be hard without Him!

*Things get hard when we try to do them independently
without leaning on and relying on God's grace.*

GOD'S WORD FOR YOU

When Pharaoh let the people go, God led them not by way of the land of the Philistines, although that was nearer; for God said, Lest the people change their purpose when they see war and return to Egypt.

EXODUS 13:17

For no temptation (no trial regarded as enticing to sin, no matter how it comes or where it leads) has overtaken you and laid hold on you that is not common to man [that is, no temptation or trial has come to you that is beyond human resistance and that is not adjusted and adapted and belonging to human experience, and such as man can bear]. But God is faithful [to His Word and to His compassionate nature], and He [can be trusted] not to let you be tempted and tried and assayed beyond your ability and strength of resistance and power to endure, but with the temptation He will [always] also provide the way out (the means of escape to a landing place), that you may be capable and strong and powerful to bear up under it patiently.

1 CORINTHIANS 10:13

136

$\mathscr{H}$IS WAY IS NOT TOO HARD

God led the Children of Israel on a longer, harder route in the wilderness because He knew they were not ready for the battles they would face in possessing the Promised Land. He needed to do a work in their lives first, teaching them Who He was and that they could not depend on themselves.

You can be assured that anywhere God leads you, He is able to keep you. He never allows more to come on us than we can bear. We do not have to live in a constant struggle if we learn to lean on Him continually for the strength we need.

If you know God has asked you to do something, don't back down because it gets hard. When things get hard, spend more time with Him, lean more on Him, and receive more grace from Him (Hebrews 4:16). Grace is the power of God coming to you at no cost, to do through you what you cannot do by yourself.

God knows that the easy way is not always the best way for us. That's why it is so important that we not lose heart, grow weary, and faint.

Satan knows that if he can defeat us in our mind,
he can defeat us in our experience.

GOD'S WORD FOR YOU

But Jesus looked at them and said, With men this is impossible, but all things are possible with God.

MATTHEW 19:26

ᗪETERMINATION

Many people I meet want to start at point A in their Christian life, blink their eyes twice, and be at point Z. Many of them are frustrated about not knowing what their gifts are or what God has called them to do with their life. Some of them are so afraid of failing and making mistakes that it keeps them from stepping out.

We all have undeveloped potential, but we will never see it manifested until we believe that we can do whatever God says we can do in His Word. Unless we step out in faith, believing that with God nothing is impossible, He cannot do the work in us that He wants to do to develop our potential. It takes our cooperation and willingness through determination, obedience, and hard work to develop what He has put in us.

Nobody can be determined for us. We must be determined. If we are not determined, the devil will steal from us everything we have. So give your potential some form by doing something with it. You will never find what you are capable of doing if you never try anything. Don't stay in the safety zone. Step out into what you feel God is leading you to do, and you will soon discover what you really can do.

Most of us have no problem with wishbone;
it's backbone that we are lacking.

GOD'S WORD FOR YOU

And let us not lose heart and grow weary and faint in acting nobly and doing right, for in due time and at the appointed season we shall reap, if we do not loosen and relax our courage and faint.

GALATIANS 6:9

Hang Tough!

Losing heart and fainting refer to giving up in the mind. The Holy Spirit tells us not to give up in our mind, because if we hold on, we will eventually reap.

Think about Jesus. Immediately after being baptized and filled with the Holy Spirit, He was led into the wilderness to be tested and tried by the devil. He did not complain and become discouraged and depressed. He did not think or speak negatively. He did not become confused trying to figure out why this had to happen! He went through each test victoriously (Luke 4:1–13).

Can you imagine Jesus traveling around the country, talking with His disciples about how hard everything was? Can you picture Him discussing how difficult the Cross was going to be . . . or how He dreaded the things ahead . . . or how frustrating it was to have no roof over His head, no bed to sleep in at night?

Jesus drew strength from His heavenly Father and came out in victory. We have His Spirit dwelling inside us and the strength available to make it through whatever we are facing.

You and I have the mind of Christ, and we can handle life situations the way He did—by being mentally prepared through "victory thinking" rather than "give up thinking."

GOD'S WORD FOR YOU

So, since Christ suffered in the flesh for us, for you, arm yourselves with the same thought and purpose [patiently to suffer rather than fail to please God]. For whoever has suffered in the flesh [having the mind of Christ] is done with [intentional] sin [has stopped pleasing himself and the world, and pleases God],

So that he can no longer spend the rest of his natural life living by [his] human appetites and desires, but [he lives] for what God wills.

1 PETER 4:1–2

Keep on Keeping On

Peter's beautiful passage teaches us a secret concerning how to make it through difficult times and situations. Here is my rendition of these verses:

"Think about everything Jesus went through and how He endured suffering in His flesh, and it will help you make it through your difficulties. Arm yourselves for battle; prepare yourselves for it by thinking as Jesus did . . . 'I will patiently suffer rather than fail to please God.' For if you suffer, having the mind of Christ toward it, you will no longer be living just to please yourself, doing whatever is easy and running from all that is hard. But you will be able to live for what God wills and not by your feelings and carnal thoughts."

There is suffering "in the flesh" that we will have to endure in order to do God's will. Trials and tests will come to develop the potential God has put in you. Your part is to determine that you are not going to quit, no matter what, until you see manifested what God has placed within you. There is one kind of person the devil can never defeat—one who is not a quitter!

Keep on keeping on, and you'll get there.

GOD'S WORD FOR YOU

*And set your minds and keep them set on what is above
(the higher things), not on the things that are on the earth.*

COLOSSIANS 3:2

$\mathscr{S}$ET YOUR MIND AND KEEP IT SET

We can have right and wrong mind-sets. The right ones benefit us, and the wrong ones hurt us and hinder our progress. We need our minds set in the right direction.

Some people see life negatively because they have experienced unhappy circumstances all their lives and can't imagine anything getting any better. Then there are some people who see everything as negative simply because their personality leans in that direction. Some people live in a wilderness of negativity, while others are a wilderness. Whatever its cause, a negative outlook leaves a person miserable and unlikely to grow spiritually.

With God's help and your hard work and determination, you can break negative mind-sets and old habits that are hurting and hindering you. The devil doesn't want you to break through because he knows that if you do, you will become a world changer. Your life will change, which will cause many other lives to change. If you develop your potential, it is going to have a positive effect not only on your life, but on someone else's life.

Your potential is a priceless treasure, like gold.
All of us have gold hidden within, but we must be
determined to dig to get it out.

GOD'S WORD FOR YOU

Wherefore seeing we also are compassed about with so great a cloud of witnesses, let us lay aside every weight, and the sin which doth so easily beset us, and let us run with patience the race that is set before us . . .

HEBREWS 12:1 KJV

Run the Race

If we are going to run our race, we must lay aside every weight and sin and run the race with patience. In the days this verse was written, runners conditioned their bodies for a race just as we do today. But at the time of the race, they stripped off their extra clothing so that when they ran there would be nothing to hinder them. They also oiled their bodies with fine oils.

In our Christian life we need to remove anything that hinders us from running the race that God has set before us. We need to be well oiled or anointed with the Holy Spirit if we are going to win our race.

The devil has a thousand ways to entangle us and prevent us from doing what we are supposed to be doing. The world we live in is filled with constant distractions. Too many commitments, letting other people control our time, not knowing how to say no, or getting overly involved in someone else's problems instead of keeping our eyes on our own goals will keep us from fulfilling our potential.

We have to be determined that nothing is going to hinder us from fulfilling God's plan and purpose for our life.

GOD'S WORD FOR YOU

Consider it wholly joyful, my brethren, whenever you are enveloped in or encounter trials of any sort or fall into various temptations.

Be assured and understand that the trial and proving of your faith bring out endurance and steadfastness and patience.

But let endurance and steadfastness and patience have full play and do a thorough work, so that you may be [people] perfectly and fully developed [with no defects], lacking in nothing.

JAMES 1:2–4

ℬE PATIENT

James teaches us that we should rejoice when we find ourselves involved in difficult situations, knowing that God is trying our faith to bring out patience. I have found that trials did eventually bring out patience in me, but first they brought a lot of other junk to the surface—such as pride, anger, rebellion, self-pity, complaining, and many other things. It seems that these ungodly traits need to be faced and dealt with before patience can come forth.

The Bible talks about purification, sanctification, sacrifice, and suffering. These are not popular words; nevertheless, if I am to become Christlike in my character, I must go through such things and learn His ways. God's desire is to make us perfect, lacking in nothing. The devil cannot control a patient person.

I struggled with the process of change for a long time, but I finally realized that God was not going to do things my way. There were people and situations He placed in my life that made me want to give up and quit. But He did not want an argument from me. He only wanted to hear, "Yes, Lord. Your will be done."

Going through difficulties instead of attempting to avoid them will save you a lot of agony.

GOD'S WORD FOR YOU

For you have need of steadfast patience and endurance, so that you may perform and fully accomplish the will of God, and thus receive and carry away [and enjoy to the full] what is promised.

HEBREWS 10:36

Therefore humble yourselves [demote, lower yourselves in your own estimation] under the mighty hand of God, that in due time He may exalt you . . .

1 PETER 5:6

WAIT ON THE LORD

There are multitudes of unhappy, unfulfilled Christians in the world simply because they are so busy trying to make something happen, instead of waiting patiently for God to bring things to pass in His own time and His own way. We are in a hurry, but God isn't.

Humility says, "God knows best, and He will not be late!" Pride says, "I'm ready now. I'll make things happen my own way." A humble man waits patiently; he actually has a "reverential fear" of moving in the strength of his own flesh. Patience is the ability to keep a good attitude while waiting. But a proud man tries one thing after another, all to no avail. Pride is at the root of impatience.

Patience is a fruit of the Holy Spirit that manifests itself in a calm, positive attitude despite our life circumstances. Don't think you can solve all your problems or overcome difficulties on your own. As we humble ourselves under God's mighty hand, we begin to die to our own way and our own timing and to become alive to God's will and way for us. Character development takes time and patience.

It is only through patience and endurance in faith that we receive the promises of God.

I WILL
HAVE FAITH

You and I need to make a decision that, come what may, we are going to keep pressing on, looking to Jesus, no matter what.

G O D ' S   W O R D   F O R   Y O U

I am calling up memories of your sincere and unqualified faith (the leaning of your entire personality on God in Christ in absolute trust and confidence in His power, wisdom, and goodness), [a faith] that first lived permanently in [the heart of] your grandmother Lois and your mother Eunice and now, I am [fully] persuaded, [dwells] in you also.

That is why I would remind you to stir up (rekindle the embers of, fan the flame of, and keep burning) the [gracious] gift of God, [the inner fire] that is in you by means of the laying on of my hands [with those of the elders at your ordination].

For God did not give us a spirit of timidity (of cowardice, of craven and cringing and fawning fear), but [He has given us a spirit] of power and of love and of calm and well-balanced mind and discipline and self-control.

2 TIMOTHY 1:5–7

t w o

I WILL HAVE FAITH

I have a feeling that in these last days we will need to be reminded of Paul's words of encouragement to Timothy of being willing to sacrifice or to suffer to fulfill the call of God on our life. Everything we have to do is not going to feel good all the time.

Timothy was a young minister who simply felt like giving up. The fire that once burned within him was beginning to grow cold. The church in those days was experiencing a great deal of persecution, and Timothy had some fears. Perhaps he felt worn out and that everything was crashing down upon him. We all feel at times that we just can't keep going.

Paul was saying, "Timothy, you may feel like quitting, but I want to see some stability in you. Remember the power of the Holy Spirit that changed your life. He gives you a spirit of discipline and self-control."

If we have stability, we do what is right when it feels good and when it doesn't feel good—whether it's praying or giving or any other obedience God is asking of us. If we ever want to see a release of our potential, we must display stability.

I don't know about you, but I have made up my mind that I will put my faith in God and His Word, come what may.

GOD'S WORD FOR YOU

But the fruit of the [Holy] Spirit [the work which His presence within accomplishes] is love, joy (gladness), peace, patience (an even temper, forbearance), kindness, goodness (benevolence), faithfulness,

Gentleness (meekness, humility), self-control (self-restraint, continence). Against such things there is no law [that can bring a charge].

GALATIANS 5:22–23

Stop the Emotional Yo-yo

I remember the years when I was what I call a "yo-yo Christian." I was continually up and down. If my husband, Dave, did what I liked, I was happy. If he didn't do what I liked, I would get mad. I was led by my emotions rather than the Holy Spirit within.

More than any other single thing, believers tell me how they feel. "I feel nobody loves me." "I feel my spouse doesn't treat me right." "I feel that I'll never be happy." "I feel . . . I feel . . . I don't feel . . . ," and on and on it goes.

God wants us to grow up and realize that our emotions are never going to go away, so we must learn to manage them rather than letting them manage us. We have to exercise self-control and tell our flesh to get in line with what is right rather than what it wants. We need to tell ourselves that we are not going to be able to say everything we want to say, eat everything we want to eat, stay up as late as we want, or get up when we feel like it. By the power of the Spirit, He will help us stop living by our emotions, and teach us to be stable.

As Christians, instead of concentrating on how we feel, we need to focus on what we know to be truth from the Word of God.

GOD'S WORD FOR YOU

Jesus Christ (the Messiah) is [always] the same, yesterday, today, [yes] and forever (to the ages).

HEBREWS 13:8

God Is Unchanging

What is the main thing that we love so much about Jesus? There are many answers to that question, of course, such as the fact that He died for us on the cross so we wouldn't have to be punished for our sins; then He rose again on the third day. But in our daily relationship with Him, one of the things we appreciate the most about Him is the fact that we can count on His unchanging nature. He can change anything else that needs to be changed, but He Himself always remains the same.

That is the kind of person I want to be, and God wants me to be, but it will never happen if I cannot control my emotions. Being emotionally mature means making decisions based on the leading of the Holy Spirit, not on our feelings. But it doesn't come naturally.

Just knowing these things is not going to make our emotions go away. But we have a God Who is able to bring us into balance. It doesn't mean we become emotionless or dull. God gave us emotions so we could enjoy life. But it does mean we take control in the strength and power of the Holy Spirit.

God does not want us to change every time our circumstances change. He wants us to always be the same, just as He is.

GOD'S WORD FOR YOU

Every good gift and every perfect (free, large, full) gift is from above; it comes down from the Father of all [that gives] light, in [the shining of] Whom there can be no variation [rising or setting] or shadow cast by His turning [as in an eclipse].

JAMES 1:17

$\mathcal{G}$OD IS ALWAYS GOOD

James tells us that God is good, period. He is not good sometimes; He is always good.

Isn't it wonderful to have a God Who is unvarying? With God there is no turning, no variation. We have seen that His Son, Jesus, never changes. In John 10:30, we are told that Jesus and God are one and the same. If Jesus never changes, God never changes. Whether in the form of the Father, His Son, Jesus, or the Holy Spirit, God is always the same.

If we are having a hard time, if we feel like giving up, God is still good. If something bad happens to us, God is still good. God is a good God, and He wants to do good things for us. He doesn't do good things for us because we are good and we deserve them; He does good things for us because He is good and He loves us.

The world still needs to learn that truth. So do some in the church. It's a revelation that can blow away doubt and fear and discouragement. It can turn darkness to light!

The key to happiness and fulfillment is not in changing our situation or circumstances, but in trusting God to be God in our life.

GOD'S WORD FOR YOU

He is the Rock, His work is perfect, for all His ways are law and justice. A God of faithfulness without breach or deviation, just and right is He.

DEUTERONOMY 32:4

For they are a nation void of counsel, and there is no understanding in them.

O that they were wise and would see through this [present triumph] to their ultimate fate!

How could one have chased a thousand, and two put ten thousand to flight, except their Rock had sold them, and the Lord had delivered them up?

For their rock is not like our Rock, even our enemies themselves judge this.

DEUTERONOMY 32:28–31

The Lord Is Our Rock

God always loves us unconditionally. He doesn't love us if we are good and then stop loving us if we are bad. He always loves us. He is always kind, always slow to anger, always full of grace and mercy, always ready to forgive.

God is a Rock, unchanging and undeviating. He is great and unfailing, faithful and just, perfect and right in all His doing. He will never leave us or forsake us.

What would happen in our lives and in the lives of those around us if we were like God? What would happen if we were always loving, always slow to anger, always filled with grace and mercy, always ready to forgive? What would happen if we, like our God, were always positive, peaceful, and generous? He is our Rock, but He is also our Example. We are to strive to be the way He is.

I know that anyone can change if I can because I had a bad case of instability. God does not expect us to become perfect overnight, but He wants to help us to become more and more like Him day by day.

God wants you to come into a place of stability.
You will never be able to enjoy life as you
were meant to until you become stable.

GOD'S WORD FOR YOU

Now when Jesus went into the region of Caesarea Philippi, He asked His disciples, Who do people say that the Son of Man is?

And they answered, Some say John the Baptist; others say Elijah; and others Jeremiah or one of the prophets.

He said to them, But who do you [yourselves] say that I am?

Simon Peter replied, You are the Christ, the Son of the living God.

Then Jesus answered him, Blessed (happy, fortunate, and to be envied) are you, Simon Bar-Jonah. For flesh and blood [men] have not revealed this to you, but My Father Who is in heaven.

And I tell you, you are Peter [Greek, Petros—a large piece of rock], and on this rock [Greek, petra—a huge rock like Gibraltar] I will build My church, and the gates of Hades (the powers of the infernal region) shall not overpower it [or be strong to its detriment or hold out against it].

MATTHEW 16:13–18

A Rock-Solid Foundation

When Peter said that Jesus was the Christ, the Son of the living God, that was a statement of faith. In making this statement, Peter was displaying faith.

I don't think Peter just casually or nonchalantly made that statement. I think he did it with a surety and a certainty that impressed Jesus because He immediately turned to Peter and told him that he was blessed. Then He went on to say that it was upon this rock-solid foundation of faith that He would build His church.

Jesus was saying to Peter, "If you maintain this faith, it will be a rocklike substance in your life upon which I will be able to build My kingdom in you. Your potential will be developed to the place that even the gates of hell will not be able to prevail against you."

There have been many times in my life when I have been discouraged and not known what to do, or felt that nothing was working and that everybody was against me. The word I have heard over and over again is, "Only believe."

This promise was not just for Peter alone.
Jesus is saying the same thing to you and me.
Only believe!

GOD'S WORD FOR YOU

For therein is the righteousness of God revealed from faith to faith: as it is written, The just shall live by faith.

ROMANS 1:17 KJV

From Faith to Faith

It has long been a goal of mine to learn how to live from faith to faith. A number of years ago the Lord revealed to me, "Joyce, you go from faith to faith to doubt to unbelief, and then back to faith to doubt to unbelief."

The trouble with the church today is that we have too much mixture and not enough stability. That mixture is evident in our speech, as we see in James 3:10: "Out of the same mouth come forth blessing and cursing. These things, brethren, ought not to be so."

Perhaps you feel as I did—like a flat tire. We get all pumped up and roll along fine for a while, but then the next thing you know we are flat again. Too often we operate at zero power level. We keep mixing positives and negatives. Our positives are deleted by our negatives, and we end up right back at zero. I don't know about you, but I don't want to operate at zero power.

It's time to determine to stop the negatives—in our thoughts, our words, and our actions.

Doubt comes in the form of thoughts that oppose the Word of God. We must determine to know the Word, then we can recognize when the devil is lying to us.

GOD'S WORD FOR YOU

Trust in, lean on, rely on, and have confidence in Him at all times, you people; pour out your hearts before Him. God is a refuge for us (a fortress and a high tower). Selah [pause, and calmly think of that]!

PSALM 62:8

I will bless the Lord at all times; His praise shall continually be in my mouth.

PSALM 34:1

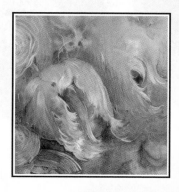

At All Times

We are not to have faith and trust in God once in a while or from time to time, but at all times. We must learn to live from faith to faith, trusting the Lord when things are good, and when things are bad. It is easy to trust God when things are good, but when things are going bad and we decide to trust God, that is when we develop character.

The psalmist also tells us we should bless the Lord at all times. There are several other Scriptures that tell us things to do at all times—resist the devil at all times, believe God at all times, love others at all times—not just when it's convenient or it feels good.

There will never come a time when we will not find temptation lurking around us. As long as we live in the flesh, we will have desires that bring hurt and damage. It is only by disciplining our emotions, our moods, and our mouths that we become stable enough to remain peaceful, whatever our situation or circumstances, so that we are able to walk in the fruit of the Spirit—whether we feel like it or not.

Since you can choose your own thoughts, when doubt comes you should learn to recognize it for what it is, say, "No, thank you," and keep on believing!

GOD'S WORD FOR YOU

But the boat was by this time out on the sea, many furlongs . . . , beaten and tossed by the waves, for the wind was against them.

And in the fourth watch [between 3:00—6:00 a.m.] of the night, Jesus came to them, walking on the sea.

And when the disciples saw Him walking on the sea, they were terrified and said, It is a ghost! . . .

But instantly He spoke to them, saying, Take courage! I AM! Stop being afraid!

And Peter answered Him, Lord, if it is You, command me to come to You on the water.

He said, Come! So Peter got out of the boat and walked on the water, and he came toward Jesus.

But when he perceived and felt the strong wind, he was frightened, and as he began to sink, he cried out, Lord, save me [from death]!

Instantly Jesus reached out His hand and caught and held him, saying to him, O you of little faith, why did you doubt?

And when they got into the boat, the wind ceased.

MATTHEW 14:24–32

*K*EEP ON WALKING

Peter stepped out at the command of Jesus to do something he had never done before. As a matter of fact, no one had ever done it except Jesus.

It required faith!

Then Peter made the mistake of spending too much time looking at the storm. He became frightened. Doubt and unbelief pressed in on him, and he began to sink. He cried out to Jesus to save him, and He did.

In Romans 4:18–21, Abraham did not waver in his faith when he considered his impossible situation. He was aware of it, but he didn't get preoccupied with it. You and I can be aware of our circumstances and yet, purposely, keep our mind on something that will build us up and edify our faith.

The devil brings storms into your life to intimidate you. We glorify God when we continue to do what we know is right even in adverse circumstances.

❧

When the storms come in your life, dig in both heels, set your face like flint, and be determined in the Holy Spirit to stay out of the boat! Very often the storm ceases as soon as you quit and crawl back into a place of safety and security.

I WILL
OVERCOME

*Just because I don't understand
what is going on in my life does not mean
God does not have a purpose for it,
or just because I don't feel good about
something does not mean it is not going
to work out for the best.*

GOD'S WORD FOR YOU

Oh, let the wickedness of the wicked come to an end, but establish the [uncompromisingly] righteous [those upright and in harmony with You]; for You, Who try the hearts and emotions and thinking powers, are a righteous God.

PSALM 7:9

But, O Lord of hosts, Who judges rightly and justly, Who tests the heart and the mind, let me see Your vengeance on them, for to You I have revealed and committed my cause [rolling it upon You].

JEREMIAH 11:20

three

I WILL OVERCOME

ll of our life is filled with constant challenges and difficulties that test our resolve and determination and the quality of our character. It would be a great mistake to overlook the fact that it is God Who tests our hearts, our emotions, and our minds.

How do we test anything? We put pressure on it to see if it will do what it says it will do. Will it hold up under stress? Can it perform at the level its maker says it can? Is it genuine when measured against a true standard of quality? God does the same with us.

It is very sad to me how many people never make it past the trying point. They lack the power of determination to pass the test and spend their whole life going around and around the same proverbial mountains. But in God's school we don't flunk. We just keep taking the test over and over until we pass it.

James 1:2–4 says that tests bring out what is in us. It is in times of trial that we become best acquainted with ourselves and what we are capable of doing. Peter didn't think he would ever deny Jesus, but he caved in when tested. As difficult as it was, that test was the step that shaped Peter into the man of God he eventually became.

God is not impressed with what we say we will do; He is impressed with what we prove we will do under pressure.

GOD'S WORD FOR YOU

[You should] be exceedingly glad on this account, though now for a little while you may be distressed by trials and suffer temptations,

So that [the genuineness] of your faith may be tested, [your faith] which is infinitely more precious than the perishable gold which is tested and purified by fire. [This proving of your faith is intended] to redound to [your] praise and glory and honor when Jesus Christ (the Messiah, the Anointed One) is revealed.

1 PETER 1:6–7

Why Be Tested?

There are many tests that come our way every day. For example, our boss tells us to do something we don't want to do. Or we're going to pull into a parking space and someone zooms in and takes it. Or someone speaks rudely to us when we've done them a favor.

In 1 Peter 4:12, Peter tells us not to be surprised or dismayed by the tests that we have to endure because by them God is testing our "quality," or our character. Peter knew the value of being tested in his own life. We all go through them, and we shouldn't be confused about why they come our way. God is testing our heart to see what manner of person we are.

Every time God gives us a test, we can tell how far we've come and how far we still have to go by how we react in that test. Attitudes of the heart that we didn't even know we had can come out when we are in tests and trials. So, Peter concludes in verse 13 that we should rejoice with triumph in our suffering so that Christ's glory may be revealed through us.

Testing times that God permits in our life are actually for our benefit, despite how we feel while we're going through them.

GOD'S WORD FOR YOU

But He knows the way that I take [He has concern for it, appreciates, and pays attention to it]. When He has tried me, I shall come forth as refined gold [pure and luminous].

JOB 23:10

I WILL TRUST GOD

One of the tests we can expect to encounter in our journey with God is the trust test. How many times do we say to God, "What is going on in my life? What are You doing? What is happening? I don't understand." Sometimes the things happening in us seem to be taking us in the exact opposite direction of what we feel God has revealed to us.

This is where many people give up and fail and go back to something that will be quicker and easier for them. If you are in a place right now where nothing in your life makes any sense, trust God anyway. One lesson I've learned through the years is this: There is no such thing as trusting God without unanswered questions. As long as God is training us to trust, there are always going to be things in our life we just don't understand.

When heaven is silent, I have learned that I need to stay busy doing the last thing God told me to do and just keep trusting Him. God will make all the pieces of our life work together for His purpose, even when we don't see tomorrow's provision. Tomorrow's answers usually don't come until tomorrow.

We must determine to trust God when we don't understand what is going on in our life.

GOD'S WORD FOR YOU

For we [Christians] are the true circumcision, who worship God in spirit and by the Spirit of God and exult and glory and pride ourselves in Jesus Christ, and put no confidence or dependence [on what we are] in the flesh and on outward privileges and physical advantages and external appearances . . .

PHILIPPIANS 3:3

I am the Vine; you are the branches. Whoever lives in Me and I in him bears much (abundant) fruit. However, apart from Me [cut off from vital union with Me] you can do nothing.

JOHN 15:5

I WILL BE SECURE IN JESUS

God despises independence. He wants us to be as totally dependent and reliant upon Him as a branch is on a vine. We are not to put confidence in the flesh, not ours or anybody else's.

How many times have you trusted in your own strength and failed miserably? How many times have other people let you down after you put your trust in them? How many times have you been disappointed when others rejected you or failed to do what you expected? God will keep taking us through these tests until we put our confidence in Him alone. The tests don't change, but we change.

Some people spend their whole lives trying to make everybody and everything else change—trying to control other people, trying to control their circumstances—without realizing the real source of their misery and unhappiness. We are in for constant failure and disappointment as long as our security is in ourselves or other people. We will be held hostage to certain things to make us happy and never get around to changing because we expect everyone and everything else to change.

We must determine to allow the tests in our lives to cause the impurities in us to rise to the top where they can be dealt with.

GOD'S WORD FOR YOU

Cease to trust in [weak, frail, and dying] man, whose breath is in his nostrils [for so short a time]; in what sense can he be counted as having intrinsic worth?

For behold, the Lord, the Lord of hosts, is taking away from Jerusalem and from Judah the stay and the staff [every kind of prop], the whole stay of bread and the whole stay of water . . .

ISAIAH 2:22—3:1

✐ WILL LEAN ON GOD

God asks us through the prophet Isaiah, "Why are you putting your trust in weak, frail, and mortal people? In what sense can they be counted on as having intrinsic worth? Instead, put your trust in Me." In light of that, He adds that He is taking away from His people all their props.

What happens to us when our props are pulled out from under us? We discover what we are really leaning on, what we are really rooted and grounded in.

As new believers in Christ, when we begin our walk with God we need a prop system, something to help us on our way. We need a group of people around us to keep us studying the Bible, praying, and seeking the Lord. Without that support system, when the storms of life come against us, they will blow us over.

That support system may take many forms, but sooner or later God is going to start removing the props from under us. At first, this is pretty scary because we don't understand it or like it. It is then we discover how much of our sense of value and worth depends on the things we are doing. Our place is to cooperate with the Lord while He does His work in our lives.

❧

We must put our roots down deep in Christ so that we can stand tall and steady and be a tree of righteousness.

GOD'S WORD FOR YOU

Remember that I told you, A servant is not greater than his master [is not superior to him]. If they persecuted Me, they will also persecute you; if they kept My word and obeyed My teachings, they will also keep and obey yours.

JOHN 15:20

He who hears and heeds you [disciples] hears and heeds Me; and he who slights and rejects you slights and rejects Me; and he who slights and rejects Me slights and rejects Him who sent Me.

LUKE 10:16

I WILL SHAKE OFF REJECTION

People will reject us just as they rejected Jesus, Paul, and the other apostles and disciples. We are servants of a rejected Master, and He leads us to do things that are different from what others around us are doing. But it is especially hard when we are rejected by people who are wrong and who are saying and doing wrong things.

When I first started preaching, I was terribly insecure and took my share of criticism and rejection. Finally, after struggling through embarrassments and feeling bad, the Lord simply said to me, "I am the One Who called you. Don't worry what people think. If you do, you are going to be worrying all your life because the devil will never stop finding people who will think something unkind about you."

In Acts 28:1–5, when Paul was bitten by a snake, the natives of the island of Malta thought he must be a murderer and their avenging goddess of justice would not allow him to live. Paul simply shook off the snake and suffered no evil effects. That is what we must do with fear, rejection, discouragement, disappointment, betrayal, or loneliness—shake it off and go on.

Even when our rejection is from people who are close to us, we must determine to keep pressing on toward fulfilling what God has called us to do.

GOD'S WORD FOR YOU

But Jesus said to him, Judas! Would you betray and deliver up the Son of Man with a kiss?

LUKE 22:48

✒ WILL NOT BE BITTER

Jesus bore our sins so we do not have to bear them. But there are other things He went through that He endured as an example for us, things that we will have to follow in His footsteps and go through. Jesus faced the betrayal of Judas at the worst moment of His life but did not let it hinder Him. And it came in the form of a kiss.

Satan loves betrayal because often when we are hurt by someone we love, respect, and trust, we feel we can't trust anyone. Think of what David felt with Absolam, or Joseph with his brothers. We want to give up and "do our own thing" so we never have to experience that hurt again. Betrayal is something we must learn to shake off and not let hinder us, no matter how we feel.

In Matthew 24:10–13, Jesus warns us that in the last days betrayals will increase. He also tells us that those who endure to the end will be saved. As believers, it is not what happens to us that ruins us. It is our wrong response to what happens that ruins us. We can choose to make a right response.

We must determine that with God's help we will allow our pain to make us better, not bitter.

187

GOD'S WORD FOR YOU

And the Lord turned the captivity of Job and restored his fortunes, when he prayed for his friends; also the Lord gave Job twice as much as he had before.

JOB 42:10

I WILL FORGIVE

One need not read far in the Bible to see the need of forgiving others. Many of the heroes of the Bible— Moses, Paul, Joseph, Stephen, Jesus, and others—had to forgive others for unthinkable hurts and wrongs.

But I will point out the case of Job, whom God told to pray for his friends who did not stand with him in his pain and suffering when he lost everything, but who judged him severely. Not only was their counsel unfair and cruel, but it was couched and twisted in spiritual words that must have pierced into Job's despair. As a result of his prayer and his forgiveness of them, Job received a double blessing from God.

The test of forgiveness comes in all sizes—from petty issues to cruelty and persecution. At whatever level, Satan knows that if we do not forgive, our faith will not work. Everything that comes from God comes by faith. And if our faith doesn't work, we are in serious trouble.

The heart of Jesus was never to return evil for evil, but to be charitable, unselfish, speaking kind words to those who harmed Him. That is His way for us.

We must determine to walk in the power of God's love and forgiveness, no matter what hatred, bitterness, or malice we may face.

GOD'S WORD FOR YOU

For if you love those who love you, what reward can you have? Do not even the tax collectors do that?

MATTHEW 5:46

I WILL LOVE

We all have a few people in our life who are like sandpaper to us. Some are like an entire package of sandpaper. It seems that when they are around, we are surrounded by sandpaper on all sides, grinding away on our rough edges.

When God first called me to preach, God put three people in my life who irritated the daylights out of me. One was my husband, Dave, who never seemed to do things the way I wanted them done. Another was a friend who was a perfectionist, who saw life in a way that drove my choleric personality crazy. The other was a girl who lived next door who was really vague about everything she wanted to do, while I felt I excelled in setting goals and being definite in everything I wanted to do. The sandpaper was grinding on me.

I thought everybody else had a problem. I resisted all the things I now know God had placed in my life. Then I discovered that God puts irritating people in our lives so we can't get away from them. If we try to run from one, two more will appear around the corner. We must learn to love and to get along with each other. Not everyone is going to be or do what we want.

We must determine to walk in the love of Christ and let Him shape us through others He brings into our lives.

I Will
Be Faithful

We must determine that we will be faithful, even when nobody knows us or seems to care what we are doing or going through. Never leave anything God has assigned you to do unless He Himself releases you from it.

GOD'S WORD FOR YOU

And let them also be tried and investigated and proved first; then, if they turn out to be above reproach, let them serve [as deacons].

1 TIMOTHY 3:10

four

I WILL BE FAITHFUL

e are all going to be tested. Count on it. There are no exceptions—everybody goes through different tests at times in their lives. But they are all open-book tests; the answers are found in the Book. No matter what we are going through, the Bible has the revelation that God has placed there for us.

We must be faithful to keep on doing what is right, even when the right thing has not happened to us yet. If we want God to work through our lives, He is going to do a work in us first. Satan attacks us in our minds, telling us lies such as, "This is not working. This is not doing you any good now, and it's never going to do you any good. You might as well give it up and go do something else." So many people quit on God right before their breakthrough.

Today's instant society is ruining people because we think everything should be easy. But godly strength, wisdom and knowledge, spiritual maturity and character are developed in us as we go through tests.

If we want to grow up in God and do what He has called us to do, we have to just settle down and be faithful. There is no "microwave maturity."

GOD'S WORD FOR YOU

Because he has set his love upon Me, therefore will I deliver him; I will set him on high, because he knows and understands My name [has a personal knowledge of My mercy, love, and kindness—trusts and relies on Me, knowing I will never forsake him, no, never].

He shall call upon Me, and I will answer him; I will be with him in trouble, I will deliver him and honor him.

With long life will I satisfy him and show him My salvation.

PSALM 91:14–16

FAITHFUL IN LONELINESS

God wants you to know that you are never alone. Satan wants you to believe you are all alone, but you are not. He wants you to believe that no one understands how you feel, but that is not true. In addition to God being with you, many believers know how you feel and understand what you are experiencing.

When you are making spiritual progress, Satan often brings affliction to discourage you and will try to make you feel alone. Several years ago I went through a very difficult time when I was separated from many people and things very dear to me. God wanted me to move on with my life, but I was not obeying Him. When I would not move, God moved me and some of the people in my life. I realize now that it was one of the best things that ever happened to me, but at the time I thought my whole world was falling apart.

Death, divorce, losing a career, or experiencing a personal injury are some of the devastating losses that people face. If you are battling loneliness and pain, draw strength from God and know that you are moving forward. He has the power to turn your mourning into joy and to comfort you in your sorrow.

*I will hope in God's love and believe
that God is always at my side.*

GOD'S WORD FOR YOU

*O God, You are my God, earnestly will I seek You;
my inner self thirsts for You, my flesh longs and is faint for
You, in a dry and weary land where no water is.*

PSALM 63:1

FAITHFUL IN THE WILDERNESS

One of the ways God tests us is by allowing us to go through dry times, times when nothing seems to minister to us or water our soul. We go to church, and we feel no different when we leave than we did when we came. Times when our prayers seem dry and the heavens are brass, times when we can't hear or feel anything from God.

I have gone through mountaintop times, and I have been through valley times. I have had dry times in my prayer life and in my praise and worship. There have been times when I could hear from God so clearly, and there have been other times when I have not heard anything at all.

I will be honest with you. I came to a point where I don't let how I feel determine whether I believe God is with me or not. I just choose to believe He is. I just love God, and that's it. I worship Him, and that's it. I pray, I believe He hears me, and that's it. I refuse to have the ups and downs I used to go through.

I will simply trust that God knows what He is doing. If I do or don't feel anything, that's fine. I will be faithful in the wilderness as well as on the mountaintop.

GOD'S WORD FOR YOU

How have you fallen from heaven, O light-bringer and daystar, son of the morning! How you have been cut down to the ground, you who weakened and laid low the nations [O blasphemous, satanic king of Babylon!]

And you said in your heart, I will ascend to heaven; I will exalt my throne above the stars of God; I will sit upon the mount of assembly in the uttermost north.

I will ascend above the heights of the clouds; I will make myself like the Most High.

ISAIAH 14:12–14

FAITHFUL TO OBEY

It was self-will that destroyed Lucifer. In exalting himself, he said, "I will," five times. God had an answer for him: " . . . you shall be brought down to Sheol (Hades), to the innermost recesses of the pit." In other words, "You will be cast down to hell."

When God asks us to do something contrary to our will, we must remember the words of Jesus: ". . . not what I will [not what I desire], but as You will and desire." This is perhaps the hardest test to pass and pass quickly. When we want something, we don't give up easily. It takes a lot of brokenness to bring us to the place where we are pliable and moldable in the hand of God.

The bottom line is that we must be willing to do whatever God says, and not what we feel or want. He may ask us to give away things we don't want to part with. He may ask us to go places, do things, and deal with people we don't want anything to do with. He may tell us to keep our mouths shut when we want to blast someone.

I will be faithful to always put God's will ahead of my own.

GOD'S WORD FOR YOU

I do not frustrate the grace of God: for if righteousness come by the law, then Christ is dead in vain.

GALATIANS 2:21 KJV

FAITHFUL WHEN FRUSTRATED

I know what frustration is like because I spent many years in frustration. I knew nothing of the grace of God. I have since learned that when I get frustrated, it is almost always because I am trying to make something happen instead of waiting on the Lord to make it happen. If I am frustrated, it is a sign that I am acting independently.

Are you frustrated with your spiritual growth? Does it seem the more you pray and seek God, the worse you get? Are you wrestling with an area of your personality that is causing you problems, or is there a specific bondage in your life that you can't break?

Frustration comes from trying to do something you cannot do. God is the only One Who can make things happen for you in your life. It will do no good to try to kick the doors down. But the minute you say, "Lord, I can't do this, so I let it go," you can almost feel the frustration lift off you by the grace of God.

I will let go and trust God
to do what only He can do.
I will let God be God.

GOD'S WORD FOR YOU

And Saul said to David, You are not able to go to fight against this Philistine. You are only an adolescent, and he has been a warrior from his youth.

And David said to Saul, Your servant kept his father's sheep. And when there came a lion or again a bear and took a lamb out of the flock,

I went out after it and smote it and delivered the lamb out of its mouth; and when it arose against me, I caught it by its beard and smote it and killed it.

Your servant killed both the lion and the bear; and this uncircumcised Philistine shall be like one of them, for he has defied the armies of the living God!

David said, The Lord Who delivered me out of the paw of the lion and out of the paw of the bear, He will deliver me out of the hand of this Philistine. And Saul said to David, Go, and the Lord be with you!

1 SAMUEL 17:33–37

FAITHFUL WHEN DISCOURAGED

When David volunteered to go and fight Goliath, no one encouraged him. Everyone, including the king, told him he was too young, too inexperienced, too small, and he didn't have the right armor. But David encouraged himself by recounting the victories God had given him in the past.

Understand this: There will be hundreds, maybe thousands, of times when Satan will come against you to discourage you. He knows you must have courage to overcome the attacks he launches against you to keep you from being faithful to fulfill God's good plan for your life. If you are discouraged, you become weak and lose the courage to move forward.

When you have to wait a long time for something, or when it seems that everything and everybody is against you, you end up tired and worn out. Sometimes you are not ready to face the discouragement that accompanies it. Say to God, "Lord, I will be faithful to You. Help me now, or I will surely sink." Then get up and go on.

I will face my discouragement and refuse to have
a pity party. I choose to be powerful in Christ
rather than pitiful in myself.

GOD'S WORD FOR YOU

So when He had finished washing their feet and had put on His garments and had sat down again, He said to them, Do you understand what I have done to you?

You call Me the Teacher (Master) and the Lord, and you are right in doing so, for that is what I am.

If I then, your Lord and Teacher (Master), have washed your feet, you ought [it is your duty, you are under obligation, you owe it] to wash one another's feet.

For I have given you this as an example, so that you should do [in your turn] what I have done to you.

JOHN 13:12–15

FAITHFUL TO SERVE

God will give us opportunity to be a servant, and then He will check our attitude to see how we're doing. Jesus gave us an example of servanthood by washing the feet of the disciples and then telling them, "You should do to others as I have done to you."

Some people fail to be servants because they don't know who they are in Christ. They feel they must be doing something important, or they don't feel they are worth anything. They fail to see the value of doing whatever they are called upon to do, regardless of how ordinary or mundane it may seem.

We need to be willing to do whatever God wants us to do, to be used in whatever way He wants to use us. The attitude of a servant should be displayed in every area of our life. The servant test is simply how we respond to the opportunities God gives us to be a blessing to others. It reveals whether we really and truly want to be like Jesus. When God anoints a person, He is anointing that person to be a servant, not to be a famous person.

I will be faithful to wash some feet today,
starting with those in my own home.

GOD'S WORD FOR YOU

No one understands [no one intelligently discerns or comprehends]; no one seeks out God.

ROMANS 3:11

Faithful When Misunderstood

There are times when our faithfulness to God will be misunderstood by people we expect to understand and comfort us. I believe there will always be those who won't understand us. People did not understand Jesus either. Nobody really understood Him or the call on His life, not even His own family.

I remember when people would say to me, "Why do you act the way you do?" I have always been a little unique. What I mean by that is, I didn't always like what other people liked, or I didn't say or do things other people thought I should. I have always been really serious, and some people didn't understand me or my personality type.

Your obedience to God may mean that you won't fit into the regular regimen of what is going on around you. You may feel out of place, and in those moments it is really confusing and disturbing to be asked by other people, "What's wrong with you? Why do you act that way?" Remember that this is simply a test of your faithfulness.

I will stand with God and do what He says, even if nobody understands, agrees with, or supports me. Jesus understands me, and He is enough.

GOD'S WORD FOR YOU

But I trusted in, relied on, and was confident in You, O Lord; I said, You are my God.

My times are in Your hands; deliver me from the hands of my foes and those who pursue me and persecute me.

PSALM 31:14–15

And lest I should be exalted above measure through the abundance of the revelations, there was given to me a thorn in the flesh, the messenger of Satan to buffet me, lest I should be exalted above measure.

For this thing I besought the Lord thrice, that it might depart from me.

And he said unto me, My grace is sufficient for thee: for my strength is made perfect in weakness. Most gladly therefore will I rather glory in my infirmities, that the power of Christ may rest upon me.

2 CORINTHIANS 12:7–9 KJV

FAITHFUL TO HIS TIMING

God does not move in our timing. He is never late, but He is usually not early either. He is often the God of the midnight hour. It is as though we are a drowning man going down for the last time, and God comes through to rescue us at the last moment.

We must learn to trust God's timing. But before we can do that, we must come to the place where we are broken before Him. Our self-will and independence must be broken before God is free to work His will in our life and circumstances.

We see how this worked in Paul's situation. While God did not give Paul the breakthrough he wanted, He gave Paul the grace, strength, and ability to endure what he was going through and still walk in the fruit of the Spirit. One level of faith gets us delivered from trials, but another level of faith takes us through trials. Personally, I don't think it takes nearly as much faith to pray and get delivered from something as it does to continue to believe in God's power when deliverance is not being manifested. It is in those testing times that we grow in faith.

I will remain faithful and trust God to work in my situation — in His perfect timing. I will not take matters into my own hands.

I Will Stay Balanced

The source of many of our problems
is often not a big spiritual issue,
but a simple, practical area that demands
our full attention. We need to be balanced
in all of our life.

GOD'S WORD FOR YOU

Be well balanced (temperate, sober of mind), be vigilant and cautious at all times; for that enemy of yours, the devil, roams around like a lion roaring [in fierce hunger], seeking someone to seize upon and devour.

1 PETER 5:8

five

I WILL STAY BALANCED

believe we live in a world that is out of balance. I also believe that most of the people in it are out of balance. Yet one of the things that we hear very little teaching about is the importance of being in balance.

The apostle Peter had several things to say on the subject. He tells us to be well-balanced and sober of mind, which means to be disciplined and serious. He also tells us to be vigilant and cautious because we have an enemy, Satan, who is out to seize upon and devour us.

In Ephesians 4:27, Paul emphasizes this same point when he tells us to control our anger, warning us, "Leave no [such] room or foothold for the devil [give no opportunity to him]."

If we are going to keep the door closed to the devil, we have to be determined to do so. He is looking for someone out of balance, someone who is paying too much attention to one area of his life and letting the other areas of his life go to pot, so to speak. We have to be determined to keep our priorities in line with God's priorities. Many times it comes down to simple, practical areas of our life that can mean the difference between keeping the door closed or not.

*The devil is always going to give us trouble,
but we must do our part to keep the door closed to him.*

GOD'S WORD FOR YOU

Now every athlete who goes into training conducts himself temperately and restricts himself in all things. They do it to win a wreath that will soon wither, but we [do it to receive a crown of eternal blessedness] that cannot wither.

1 CORINTHIANS 9:25

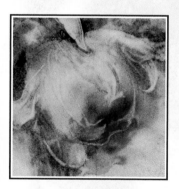

$\mathcal{R}$ESTRICT YOURSELF

First Corinthians 9:25 says that everyone who strives for mastery in anything must restrict himself in all things. This is all about the power of determination to keep our lives in balance.

Balance is not something we get into one time and stay there forever. We can be in balance on Monday and out of balance by Wednesday. It must be kept and maintained.

Nor is balance achieved over everything at once. There are thousands of areas of our life, and each one of them has to be brought into balance and then kept that way through regular maintenance and care.

We have a practical, natural side of our life that we must take care of. If we don't, it will end up hurting our spiritual side. For example, if we don't take care of our physical body, we will get sick. When we get sick, we don't feel like praying, releasing our faith, or believing the Lord. Satan looks for ways to get us out of balance so he can stop us from doing what God has called us to do.

When we have a problem, it is not always a spiritual area that is out of line. Many times it is a natural area that we are not paying attention to.

GOD'S WORD FOR YOU

*By much slothfulness the building decayeth; and
through idleness of the hands the house droppeth through.*

ECCLESIASTES 10:18 KJV

Balance in Your Work

We have all been given powers and abilities. But we have to regulate the different areas of our life to keep them in proper perspective. If we have too much work and not enough rest, we get out of balance. We become workaholics and end up burned out.

I get a lot of satisfaction out of accomplishments and work. I don't like a lot of what I consider silliness and wasted time in my life. But because of my nature, I tend to get out of balance in this area. I have to determine that I will not only work but also rest. That is a priority for me.

But it is possible to go to the extreme and have too much rest and not enough work. Solomon says that "through indolence the rafters [of state affairs] decay and the roof sinks in, and through idleness of the hands the house leaks." In other words, people who don't work enough end up in trouble. Their houses, cars, bodies, and everything else become a mess because they don't do the work necessary to keep things in order. They fail to regulate the powers at their disposal. They are out of balance.

Bring order and balance to your life one step at a time.
God is changing you day by day as you trust Him.

GOD'S WORD FOR YOU

*Of what use is money in the hand of a [self-confident]
fool to buy skillful and godly Wisdom—when he has no
understanding or heart for it?*

PROVERBS 17:16

Balance in Your Finances

We have the power to spend money or to save money. Some people try to save all their money. Either they are greedy or they are fearful about the future, thinking that money might save them from some unforeseen calamity. So they get out of balance.

Others get out of balance with money by over-spending all the time. When that happens, they start using credit cards and running them up to the maximum allowed. Some of them try to get out of debt by rebuking "the devils of debt." They want a miracle to correct their lack of discipline.

Too often that is our problem. We get ourselves into a mess and then try to get ourselves out by some miraculous method. We go from one mess to another, never wanting to take responsibility for our own mistakes. It is walking in stupidity to spend our lives ignoring the consequences of bad choices.

If you are in financial trouble, you must determine to pay off your debts. It will require great discipline and perhaps some pain, but this is not a time to feel sorry for yourself. Taking responsibility to solve the problem is for you to do.

It takes time to get into debt, and it takes time to get out of debt. Cooperate with God in dealing with it.

GOD'S WORD FOR YOU

Do you not know that your body is the temple (the very sanctuary) of the Holy Spirit Who lives within you, Whom you have received [as a Gift] from God? You are not your own . . .

1 CORINTHIANS 6:19

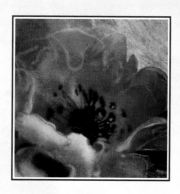

BALANCE IN YOUR DIET

If I don't determine to stick to a sensible diet, I will find something I like and eat it all the time. Of course, that is not wise because the human body was never meant to live off of sweets and snacks. We cannot eat only ice cream, candy bars, and potato chips and expect to stay healthy.

There is nothing worse than going through life feeling bad all the time. As a person who struggled for years with eating and weight problems, I know the feeling all too well. When we eat the wrong foods and put on extra pounds, we just don't feel right.

God calls each of us to do something special in this life. But to do it, we must determine to take care of our body—the house we live in. We have to find balance in what we eat and drink, get enough rest and exercise, and keep our weight down to what is right for our frame.

I don't think that anyone will be healthy without following a balanced diet. Each of us needs to know our body, what it needs, and what is really best for it. Determine today that you will begin to eat better and live free.

You are free to follow the leading of the Holy Spirit and free from doing everything your flesh demands.

GOD'S WORD FOR YOU

For God did not give us a spirit of timidity (of cowardice, of craven and cringing and fawning fear), but [He has given us a spirit] of power and of love and of calm and well-balanced mind and discipline and self-control.

2 TIMOTHY 1:7

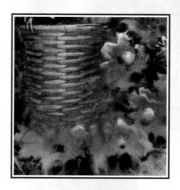

Balance in Everything

It's possible to go overboard in any area of our life. A woman can ruin her marriage by getting excessively involved in spiritual activities, such as praying and Bible studies. If she fails to pay attention to her husband's needs, no amount of spiritual reasons will compensate for the damage to her relationship.

Men have a great need for recreation and want to have fun. For some men, that need is turned into an obsession that consumes them.

Some people don't think enough, while others think too much. Some don't talk enough, and some talk too much. Some people plan too much, and some don't plan enough. Sometimes we think too highly of ourselves, and sometimes we think too lowly of ourselves. We can spend too much time on ourselves, becoming selfish and self-centered. But we can also ignore ourselves and our own needs so much that it causes deep emotional problems. Sometimes we all need to do just a little something for ourselves.

God is merciful and works with us to bring order to our lives. Take whatever steps and make whatever adjustments He is showing you.

GOD'S WORD FOR YOU

Moses' father-in-law said to him, The thing that you are doing is not good.

You will surely wear out both yourself and this people with you, for the thing is too heavy for you; you are not able to perform it all by yourself.

EXODUS 18:17–18

You Are Not Invincible

It would not surprise me to learn that God is saying the same thing to you that He said to Moses. It is a word for today. Sometimes we like to think we are invincible. We don't like anybody to tell us that something is too much for us to handle, and we push on and on despite what we feel.

I was always the kind of person who thought I could do anything I set my mind to. I was thoroughly convinced I could do all things through Christ Who strengthens me. If someone told me differently, it just made me more determined. I found out that if we have an attitude that we can do anything, no matter what it is, we are out of balance. It took some health problems to prove it to me.

Here's the truth: God does not give us power for anything He does not tell us to do. God does not give us more than we can stand or endure. If He gives us a job to do, then He gives us the ability to perform it. And I don't mean just dragging ourselves around half dead all the time. God means for you to have life and to have it abundantly.

Are there any adjustments you need to make in order to keep yourself in balance? If you will adjust, as Moses did, you will slam the door in the devil's face.

GOD'S WORD FOR YOU

But he himself went a day's journey into the wilderness and came and sat down under a lone broom or juniper tree and asked that he might die. He said, It is enough; now, O Lord, take away my life; for I am no better than my fathers.

As he lay asleep under the broom or juniper tree, behold, an angel touched him and said to him, Arise and eat.

He looked, and behold, there was a cake baked on the coals, and a bottle of water at his head. And he ate and drank and lay down again.

The angel of the Lord came the second time and touched him and said, Arise and eat, for the journey is too great for you.

So he arose and ate and drank, and went in the strength of that food forty days and nights to Horeb, the mount of God.

1 KINGS 19:4–8

GET SOME REST

Why in the world would a man such as Elijah, who on the previous day had triumphed over 450 prophets of Baal, suddenly allow himself to become so intimidated by the threats of a solitary woman named Jezebel that he ran away in fear?

If you study the story closely, it's clear that he was totally worn out and exhausted from pushing himself so hard for so long. Even an extraordinary anointing of the Spirit does not mean you won't get tired. Elijah's body was completely broken down, and his emotions had totally fallen apart. He was not handling himself the way he normally would. He was afraid, depressed, discouraged, and suicidal.

Nothing in life looks good to us when we are exhausted. It seems to us that nobody loves us, nobody helps us, nobody is concerned about us. We feel abused, misused, misunderstood, and mistreated. Many times when we feel we have deep problems, all that is wrong with us is that we are exhausted.

The Lord said to Elijah, "You're worn out. You need a couple of hot meals and a good night's rest." We need to listen to that word.

Many of the problems people have in relationships today are the result of imbalance—just being worn out.

GOD'S WORD FOR YOU

I am the True Vine, and My Father is the Vinedresser. Any branch in Me that does not bear fruit [that stops bearing] He cuts away (trims off, takes away); and He cleanses and repeatedly prunes every branch that continues to bear fruit, to make it bear more and richer and more excellent fruit. . . .

When you bear (produce) much fruit, My Father is honored and glorified, and you show and prove yourselves to be true followers of Mine.

JOHN 15:1–2, 8

ᗪETERMINE TO PRUNE

Lack of balance hinders fruitful living. And if there is anything that God wants us to do, it is to bear fruit. The first thing God said to Adam and Eve was, "Be fruitful." Jesus made it clear in John 15 that He desires us to be fruit-bearing disciples.

Jesus says that if we do not bear fruit, God will prune us to make us productive. And if we do bear fruit, God will prune us so we bear more, richer, and more excellent fruit. To us the word *prune* is a nasty, ugly word because it means to "cut away," "trim off," or "take away." Nobody likes those cutting words. But it's clear that we are going to be pruned.

God may have to clip off some things in our lives that we would like to baby and nurse along. It may mean letting go of things we're doing that we're very comfortable with. It may mean significant change to adjust to. But God knows what He has in mind for us overall. When He starts dealing with us to let go of something, the best thing we can do is just let it go because He knows His business.

When we are determined to give up our way of doing things and accept God's way of doing things, we are on the road to becoming all that God wants us to be.

I WILL
PRESS ON

God is on your side, and if He is for you, it really does not matter who is against you. The giants may be big, but God is bigger. You may have weaknesses, but God has strength. You may have sin in your life, but God has grace. You may fail, but God remains faithful!

GOD'S WORD FOR YOU

Now to Him Who, by (in consequence of) the [action of His] power that is at work within us, is able to [carry out His purpose and] do superabundantly, far over and above all that we [dare] ask or think [infinitely beyond our highest prayers, desires, thoughts, hopes, or dreams] . . .

EPHESIANS 3:20

six

I WILL PRESS ON

od loves to use common, ordinary, everyday people who have uncommon goals and visions.

That is what I am—just a common, ordinary person with a goal and vision that fuel my determination. But just because I am common and ordinary does not mean that I am content to be average. I don't like that word. I don't want to be average. I don't intend to be average. I don't serve an average God; therefore, I don't believe I have to be average—and neither do you.

I believe that anyone can be mightily used by God. I believe that we can do great and mighty things, things that amaze even us, if we believe that God can use us and if we will be daring and determined enough to have an uncommon goal and vision. By uncommon I mean something that we truly have to believe God for— beyond all that we could dare to hope, ask, or think, according to His great power that is at work in us. We need to be daring in our faith and in our prayers.

We must determine to stretch our faith into new realms. We need to be common people with uncommon goals.

GOD'S WORD FOR YOU

For [simply] consider your own call, brethren; not many [of you were considered to be] wise according to human estimates and standards, not many influential and powerful, not many of high and noble birth.

[No] for God selected (deliberately chose) what in the world is foolish to put the wise to shame, and what the world calls weak to put the strong to shame.

And God also selected (deliberately chose) what in the world is lowborn and insignificant and branded and treated with contempt, even the things that are nothing, that He might depose and bring to nothing the things that are,

So that no mortal man should [have pretense for glorying and] boast in the presence of God.

1 CORINTHIANS 1:26–29

CHOSEN BY GOD

Paul tells us plainly what God chooses and why. He says that He chooses what to the world is foolish to put the wise to shame, and what the world calls weak to put the strong to shame.

I am so glad it tells me that God deliberately chose me. He didn't get me by accident. I wasn't just pushed off on Him so that He had no choice but to carry on this ministry through me because He couldn't get anyone else to do it.

When God got the idea for Life In The Word Ministries, He looked around for the biggest mess He could find, someone who loved Him and had a right heart toward Him, someone who would work hard, someone who was determined, diligent, and disciplined. But I had no special talent. The only thing I do really well is talk, but even my voice is a bit unusual.

People look at the exterior, but God looks at the heart. His choice is not based on appearance, education, our possessions, or even our talents. It is based on our heart attitude, whether we are willing to fulfill a handful of qualifications to be used by God.

If we continue being faithful to God, we will eventually get where God wants us to be.

GOD'S WORD FOR YOU

I appeal to you therefore, brethren, and beg of you in view of [all] the mercies of God, to make a decisive dedication of your bodies [presenting all your members and faculties] as a living sacrifice, holy (devoted, consecrated) and well pleasing to God, which is your reasonable (rational, intelligent) service and spiritual worship.

ROMANS 12:1

BE USABLE

If you are a believer, your life has been consecrated to God, set apart for His use only. You don't belong to yourself, because you have been bought with a price (1 Corinthians 6:20). You have the brand of the Holy Spirit upon you (Ephesians 4:30), just as a rancher brands his cattle to show that they belong to him.

We should not have the attitude that God belongs to us and try to tell Him what we want and how He should go about getting it for us. We should not start every morning by giving God our twelve-part want list of what it is going to take to make us happy. But I spent years doing that. I used to pray, "Oh, God, if I don't have more money, I just can't stand it." Those were the wilderness years for my life.

Our problem is that too often we think about what we cannot do rather than what we can do. Whatever God requires of us, we can do. What He requires of us is simply to be usable, and all of us can do that. We can work hard, walk in wisdom, and try to make sure that our words and thoughts are pleasing to God while we trust Him to work out His good plan for our life.

We may not be able to do everything, but we can finish what God gives us to start. We can stay on the narrow path. We can be committed and disciplined.

GOD'S WORD FOR YOU

For I know the thoughts and plans that I have for you, says the Lord, thoughts and plans for welfare and peace and not for evil, to give you hope in your final outcome.

JEREMIAH 29:11

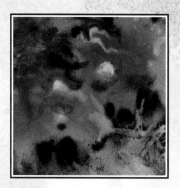

GOD HAS A PLAN

The most important thing is not how we start but how we finish. Some people get started with a bang, but they never finish. Others are slow starters, but they finish strong.

God has a plan for each of us. It is our destiny. But it is a possibility, not a "positively." Even if someone prophesies over us wonderful things in the name of the Lord, just as a prophet did with me, what is being prophesied is the heart, the will, and the desire of God for us. It doesn't mean it is positively going to happen, because if we don't cooperate with God, it is not going to come to pass. We have a part to play in seeing that plan come true. God cannot do anything in our lives without our cooperation.

I challenge you to cooperate with God every single day of your life to develop your potential. Every day you should learn something new. Every day you should grow. Every day you should be a bit further along than you were the day before.

We must each discover our own God-given gifts and talents, what we are truly capable of, and then put ourselves to the task of developing those gifts, talents, and capabilities to their fullest extent.

GOD'S WORD FOR YOU

Do not be conformed to this world (this age), [fashioned after and adapted to its external, superficial customs], but be transformed (changed) by the [entire] renewal of your mind [by its new ideals and its new attitude], so that you may prove [for yourselves] what is the good and acceptable and perfect will of God, even the thing which is good and acceptable and perfect [in His sight for you].

ROMANS 12:2

Go Against the Flow

John Mason wrote two very good books that I recommend you read. One is entitled *An Enemy Called Average*, and the other is titled *Conquering an Enemy Called Average*. One expression of his that I really like is this: "Know your limits, then ignore them." That's what I do. I know what I can't do and what I can do. I have decided to concentrate on what I can do, not what I can't do.

Too many people concentrate on everything they do wrong and never on what they do right. They get so caught up in their mistakes that they lose sight of the fact that we serve a great God. Sometimes our own inabilities distract us from looking to Jesus.

Mason also says, "The most unprofitable item ever manufactured is an excuse." People make up excuses for why they don't do anything. "I can't. It's too hard." Mother Teresa went to India with three pennies and God, and she didn't do badly.

Take an inventory. What are you doing with your time, energy, talents, abilities, and life? Are you just following everybody else? Go against the flow!

If you can only do one thing, make up your mind
that you are going to do that one thing well.
Be the best at that one thing you can do.

GOD'S WORD FOR YOU

Therefore He says, Awake, O sleeper, and arise from the dead, and Christ shall shine (make day dawn) upon you and give you light.

Look carefully then how you walk! Live purposefully and worthily and accurately, not as the unwise and witless, but as wise (sensible, intelligent people),

Making the very most of the time [buying up each opportunity], because the days are evil.

Therefore do not be vague and thoughtless and foolish, but understanding and firmly grasping what the will of the Lord is.

EPHESIANS 5:14–17

Know What You're Doing

Do you know what the will of God is for you? Do you have a vision that fuels the power of your determination? Do you know what you are going to do with your life? You should.

Now obviously, if you're just starting out on the Christian walk, you may not know your future. But God will give you something to start doing, and it will become clearer as you obey each step. But if you are forty or fifty years old, you should know God's will for your life.

I got ahold of this passage in Ephesians many years ago when God first called me into the ministry. In those days I was such a mess that I would sit on my couch after I had put the kids down for a nap and cry for two hours. That is all I knew to do back then. I was mad at Dave, had a chip on my shoulder, and had many other problems as well. Yet I was teaching a home Bible study and I loved God, and it was the will of God. It was my starting spot.

Paul tells us that we should not be vague about God's will, but we should understand and firmly grasp it.

We need to be people of purpose. We need to know why we are doing what we are doing and not lose sight of our goal.

GOD'S WORD FOR YOU

Also [Jesus] told them a parable to the effect that they ought always to pray and not to turn coward (faint, lose heart, and give up).

LUKE 18:1

ℛEFUSE TO GIVE UP

It is easy to drift backward, but we must press forward. Effortless living is never effective. Everyone thinks that the more we can get ahold of with no effort, the better life is, but that is a lie.

One thing that is wrong with us Americans today, even with our health, is the fact that we don't have much of anything to do but go through life pushing buttons—the elevator, the dishwasher, the washing machine. Just push a button and away we go. Still we gripe and grumble because we have to load and unload the machines!

We were not created to have an effortless life. We were created for work, involvement, participation, and struggle. We are not supposed to struggle with everything, but we are also not supposed to be the kind of people who quit and give up easily.

There are numerous examples of people in the Bible who simply refused to give up. Zacchaeus could not be kept from Jesus, despite his shortcomings. The woman with the issue of blood pressed through the crowd and was rewarded for her determination. This is how we reach our objectives.

The apostle Paul said that the most important thing he did was to forget what lies behind and press on.

GOD'S WORD FOR YOU

In the fourth year of Jehoiakim son of Josiah king of Judah, this word came to Jeremiah from the Lord:

Take a scroll [of parchment] for a book and write on it all the words I have spoken to you against Israel and Judah and all the nations from the day I spoke to you in the days of [King] Josiah until this day.

JEREMIAH 36:1–2

⚘ IT AGAIN!

When Jeremiah wrote this scroll, he was actually under house arrest. Certain people could visit him, but he couldn't go out. He was still receiving prophecies from the Lord and writing them down. Then one of his servants would come and carry the message throughout the land. God is not put off by inconveniences; He always finds another way to get His work done.

God gave Jeremiah a prophecy about Israel and Judah and ordered him to record it. Writing in the days of quill and ink on a scroll was a tedious job, and if copies were needed, it was long and painstaking. When the king heard about the scroll and had it brought to the royal palace and read to him, he didn't like what it said. The king enjoyed his unrighteous lifestyle, and he didn't want to change. So he cut up and burned the scroll page after page until it was all gone.

After all that, what was God's response? "Jeremiah, go get yourself another scroll and write the thing over" (see Jeremiah 36:27–28). In other words, do it again.

❧

Until we get a breakthrough and finish what God has called us to do, we need to be willing to do it again and again and again.

GOD'S WORD FOR YOU

Enter through the narrow gate; for wide is the gate and spacious and broad is the way that leads away to destruction, and many are those who are entering through it.

But the gate is narrow (contracted by pressure) and the way is straitened and compressed that leads away to life, and few are those who find it.

MATTHEW 7:13–14

Stay on the Narrow Path

Jesus made it clear that it is easy to succumb to temptation, to fall into sin, and be destroyed. It is easy to get into the flow of the world and just float along in the worldly boat with everybody else. The world is full of compromisers today, people who are willing to make any concession and live the status quo, be average, and just get by in life.

You who have gone through the narrow gate are going to have to stand against pressure. If you are determined to talk right, act right, think right, put your money in the right place, and to stop living a selfish life, Satan is not going to make it easy for you. He hates it when we decide to be radical for God.

We resist the devil by submitting to God and staying on the narrow path. Satan may tell you that you are the only one who is going through trials and tribulations and it's all worthless. The truth is, I don't know too many people who are not going through something.

Keep in mind where the narrow path leads, and you'll never give in.

Sometimes the only people you are going to find on the narrow path are you and the Lord. If that's so, just keep going!

JOYCE
MEYER

Joyce Meyer has been teaching the Word of God since 1976 and in full-time ministry since 1980. She is the bestselling author of more than fifty inspirational books, including *How to Hear from God, Knowing God Intimately,* and *Battlefield of the Mind.* She has also released thousands of teaching cassettes and a complete video library. Joyce's *Enjoying Everyday Life* radio and television programs are broadcast around the world, and she travels extensively conducting conferences. Joyce and her husband, Dave, are the parents of four grown children and make their home in St. Louis, Missouri.

Additional copies of this book are available from your local bookstore.

If this book has changed your life, we would like to hear from you.

To contact the author, write:
Joyce Meyer Ministries
P. O. Box 655 • Fenton, Missouri 63026

or call: (636) 349-0303

Internet Address: www.joycemeyer.org

In Canada, write: Joyce Meyer Ministries Canada, Inc.
Lambeth Box 1300 • London, ON N6P 1T5

or call: (636) 349-0303

In Australia, write: Joyce Meyer Ministries-Australia
Locked Bag 77 • Mansfield Delivery Centre
Queensland 4122

or call: (07) 3349 1200

In England, write: Joyce Meyer Ministries
P. O. Box 1549 • Windsor • SL4 1GT
or call: 01753 831102